MODELLING
BR TODAY

Chris Ellis

LONDON
IAN ALLAN LTD

MODELLING BR TODAY

Contents

First published 1984

ISBN 0 7110 1375 6

© Ian Allan Ltd 1984

Published by Ian Allan Ltd, Shepperton, Surrey; and printed by Ian Allan Printing Ltd at their works at Coombelands in Runnymede, England.

Previous page:
Excellent modelling of the modern BR scene by Malcolm Carlsson, as a detailed Lima Class 33 moves away from Poltreath station on the North Cornwall line, an imaginary BR branch line in the West of England. The coaches are Lima Mk 2B models converted to Mk 2D&F air conditioned stock. *Malcolm Carlsson*

Below:
N gauge lends itself particularly well to the modelling of modern BR where true scale length trains can be duplicated. Here a Deltic loco hauled express departs from the main station on the N gauge layout of Mrs Dawn Marler. *Brian Monaghan*

Introduction

An enduring love affair with steam trains amongst British modellers and enthusiasts ensured that for many years any modelling activity involving diesel or electric traction was dismissed almost derisively as 'modern image' and modellers and manufacturers tended to concentrate on reproducing the nostalgic era when steam trains reigned supreme. There have always been modellers attracted by the rail activity they see around them, however; it was usually the case in steam days, as it happens, but now, after some years when modern British Rail was not widely modelled, there are signs of greatly increased interest, probably because there is now a whole generation of young modellers who do not remember any other trains than those they see in BR blue and grey which is the period covered by this book. Manufacturers are realising the interest too, and there is an ever increasing output of good ready-to-run models. For the modeller with only limited time, skill or money, or any combination of these, modelling modern BR has much to commend itself. First of all the real thing can easily be seen in action and experienced at first hand, and on

the spot research is possible. Many operations are greatly simplified today, which can be reflected in fairly simple track layouts (even single track main lines are possible) and quite short trains if the right sort of working is chosen. All of this is good news for modellers with limited space. Then, again, it is all getting very colourful, more so as time goes on, and it is pleasing to get away from the drab greys, browns, and blacks which have predominated in the past. There is plenty to challenge the interest and imagination, indeed the subject is larger than can be incorporated even in this generously illustrated book.

Therefore I have concentrated on matters which the average modeller can pursue. Thus

there is no great coverage of Southern Region electric trains, not because they are not interesting but because at the time of writing there is little available for modellers who depend on ready-to-run and conversions for most of their activity. No doubt the gaps in model coverage will be filled as time goes on, but this book has concentrated on what can be done with material to hand at the time of writing.

There are not many layout samples given in this book because most existing 'steam age' published track plans can be used, suitably simplified and personal research will suggest ideas and features which can be incorporated into a modern layout. For those who want something definite to copy, however, I have included a personal favourite, Coombe Junction, which reflects a lot of the character of modernised BR including a simple track layout. This layout could be built along one wall, so assisting those who do not have much space at their disposal. Similarly I have omitted a section on road transport because most of the firms making model cars and commercial vehicles offer a good selection of current or recent types and finding these is the least of your problems — they can be purchased in most model and toy shops. Checking that they are to the correct scale is the main requirement as many of these items come in random sizes, which are far removed from the recognised model railway scales.

Acknowledgements
For providing photographs and information I would like to thank Allan Dare, Michael Andress, Helen M. Jerome, John Reed, Don Jones, R. Coffin, Brian Monaghan and Richard Gardner. Photographs not otherwise credited are my own. Richard Gardner also provided the Coombe Junction plans from his own research. Thanks also to Jane Cartwright for typing the manuscript.

Below:
A very nicely detailed Lima Class 33 diesel model which has been extensively rebuilt using cast and etched parts from the specialist suppliers. The body has been reduced by 2mm to make it scale width and it has much added detail such as steel handrails, flush glazing, screw couplings, scale size buffers, pipes, cables and windscreen wipers.
Malcolm Carlsson

1 Modern Image or Contemporary?

Back in what are now thought of as the 'golden days' of the model railway hobby's development — the 1930s to the 1950s — when Hornby gauge O tinplate models and Hornby-Dublo represented the best commercial standard of the day, virtually every new model in ready-to-run form reproduced contemporary practice. If the Gresley 'A4' Pacific represented the most dramatic form of express passenger power, and captured the imagination of the mass market, an 'A4' model was every youngster's dream. And so it went with other types of model. Even the miniature stations from firms like Trix and Hornby-Dublo depicted the stark stucco and concrete architectural styles of the 1930s and 1940s. Nobody in the mass market of those days thought it out of the ordinary to have available only ready-to-run models of the then current era. Anybody who wanted anything 'old time' had to build it from scratch and the articles in model railway journals of those days indicate that most modellers thought and modelled in contemporary terms. And well they might, for those were days of steam power when railways offered vast varieties of locomotives, stock and practices. It was all considered very exciting and the desire to model railways of the past was rarely detected among the mass of modellers. This state of affairs continued into the 1960s, so that new locomotive models of BR standard types became the latest releases, again keeping pace with contemporary events.

This predictable pattern was broken with the demise of steam on British Railways in the late 1960s. Nostalgic affection for steam traction divided model railway enthusiasts (and the model railway trade) into two distinct groups. There was still a big demand for 'steam age' models and in the years that followed these were the models which the public largely got, long after steam trains had disappeared from all the BR tracks. Those who preferred to model the contemporary scene — by then all diesel and electric — had a thin time of it. For though all the main mass-market manufacturers produced a few contemporary types, the bulk of their offerings continued to cover models of the steam age.

The model railway market grew considerably in the late 1960s and the 1970s, and still the trend was towards nostalgic steam from both the mass-market manufacturers and the strongly increasing ranks of specialist kit and model makers. Right into the late 1970s this trend has continued and in any typical year, so far, releases of 'steam age' models have tended to outnumber new models of contemporary types.

At times it seemed that the modeller wishing to reproduce the up-to-date scene was rather out on a limb. The term 'modern image' was coined in sections of the model railway press to describe modelling the contemporary scene, rather as if anyone who dealt in diesel and electric traction were a class apart. Some articles covering the current scene were published, it's true, but the bulk of model projects and articles tended to be related to the 'good old days' of the steam age.

In recent years, however, there has been a definite increase of interest in the modern diesel and electric scene; the steam age nostalgia has weakened, but a most important factor is the arrival of a new generation of young enthusiasts who have grown up since the 'steam age' disappeared. These are the modellers who have only seen BR blue colour schemes, who know only diesel multiple-units and the throb of a Sulzer motor in an idling diesel loco. To these modern enthusiasts steam is just a rather remote form of traction, seen on film, or experienced on the various preserved lines — but not the stuff of everyday experience.

Obviously the sheer size of the model railway hobby has increased greatly in the past decade. New manufacturers have entered the field in both the ready-to-run and kit categories. In recent years this has led to a healthy increase in the release of kits and models covering the recent or contemporary scene, and though there are gaps in the market in terms of the lists of available models, it is certainly now possible for anyone to come up with a very

Right:

Modern diesels can be as dramatic as steam, as Deltic No 55005 *The Prince of Wales's Own Regiment of Yorkshire* **demonstrates as it moves out from York round the curve at Clifton with the 08.50 Plymouth-Edinburgh train. The Deltic has just come on to the train for the run to Edinburgh. The curve gives a model layout effect, but the locomotive itself, pictured in 1980 is now part of railway history for the Deltics were all withdrawn by 1982 in favour of HSTs.** *John Chalcraft*

Deltic No 55002, now preserved in the National Railway Museum at York, painted in the old BR green in which it ran in revenue traffic until withdrawn. It is sometimes used on enthusiasts' specials and gives the modeller the excuse for running a contrasting green loco among the blue ones. *Colin J. Marsden*

Right:
There are still gaps in both the kit and ready-to-run range for the modern modeller. At the time of writing for instance, there is no model of the Class 455 EMU. The front end of these BR units is the same as the Class 317 EMUs (Bedpan units) on the Bedford-St Pancras line and the Class 210 DMUs. *David Brown*

Below right:
The same remark above applies to the Class 313 Great Northern suburban (with same body as Class 508 on SR or Class 507 on Merseyside) EMUs. This view shows one of the four-coach units at Welwyn Garden City in April 1977. *J. A. Howie*

Far right, top:
A few items of EMU stock are available in kit form, including Southern Region units. This is a partly completed SR electric motor parcels van from a Westdale kit in 7mm scale, O gauge.

Far right, bottom:
The more dramatic items of BR stock are readily available in ready-to-run form. The Class 87 and the Mk 3 coaches shown here on a Euston-Glasgow express are modelled in 4mm scale by Lima (loco) and Graham Farish (coaches) in N scale. Note the dirt on the front of the loco. *John Chalcraft*

representative collection of models for a modern style layout, at least in the three major scales and gauges — OO, N and O. Among modellers there is definitely more interest in the modern scene and the doldrum years are past when, for example, there was not on the market a single model of a diesel multiple-unit — Britain's most commonly seen passenger train. Of course, it may well be that the lack of ready-to-run models has dampened interest and for many years the real British Rail, beset with financial and industrial troubles got a rather bad press, which may not have encouraged modellers to want to reproduce the system in miniature! However, in the last few years the advent of the InterCity HST, undisputably a commercial and technical success, brighter colours on freight stock (and interesting new wagons too) plus other similar developments have made British Rail an exciting operation again and this has clearly rubbed off on enthusiasts and given them the urge to reproduce it in miniature. But above all it is the increased availability of models in the ready-to-run ranges which has done the trick. Now, it seems, the leading manufacturers have settled down to the business of supplying both the nostalgic 'steam age' market and the modellers who want to reproduce the modern British Rail scene. There are gaps a-plenty, but there's big potential too — as we shall see later in this book.

Before we get too far into the subject, however, we had better put paid to the term 'modern image' which is a convenient journalistic description but a questionable one. It came into being when steam traction was going out and diesel and electric traction was coming in — about 20 years ago now.

But there is always 'modern image', if you think of it as the contemporary scene. When the Hornby-Dublo 'A4' *Sir Nigel Gresley* first appeared in OO gauge in 1938 it was very much 'modern image' (the exact equivalent of today's HST in fact, and even described as a High Speed Train by Gresley himself). Today, it is part of 'steam age' nostalgia though happily for the model railway hobby miniature 'A4s' are still very much in demand and very much available. What was thought of as modern image when this somewhat derisive term first appeared in the model railway press is also past history — 'diesel age' archaeology, now, comprising such types as the Midland Pullman and 'Warship' diesel-hydraulic locomotives. So it

is better, perhaps, to forget the term 'modelling modern image' and merely regard yourself as modelling the contemporary scene — for this is always moving forward and you can take the cut-off point back in time to suit yourself, though the modeller who wants to create a convincing layout will obviously avoid items completely out of period. It would look wrong, for example, to have a Midland Pullman set of the 1960s running with an HST set of the late 1970s though in their respective decades each was definitely 'modern image'.

Just what approach you can take we'll discuss later, but first let us look at the historical perspective and see how the contemporary British Rail emerged.

2 Modern BR in Perspective

The real starting point for the British Rail scene as it exists today was the appointment of Dr Richard (now Lord) Beeching to the chairmanship of the newly-constituted British Railways Board (formerly the British Transport Commission) in early 1963. Beeching was given the task, by the government of the day, of reorganising the existing BR system to make the most economical use of its resources, to reduce its losses, to make it run on more commercial lines and to make it more suited to modern requirements.

The 'Beeching Axe' became part of the language, for the new Chairman did a vigorous job of reorganisation, cutting out many branch and secondary lines which did not pay, and reducing duplicated routes inherited from the pre-nationalisation days of competing companies. Though remembered for the 'Axe' which dominated the press headlines, the Beeching era was much more positively devoted to modernisation of the entire BR system, to lift it finally from the 'steam age' and its links with the old pre-nationalisation companies into a unified new organisation.

In the remaining years of the 1960s, therefore, some quite radical changes came about. The word 'rationalisation' became common currency in railway planning. The unremunerative branch lines were swept away, often to howls of protest from enthusiasts — though a few of the lines had a new lease of life as privately run preservation companies. Hence we have an interesting side line worth remembering when modelling the modern era — preserved steam lines. Some, like the Bluebell Railway (one of the first), the Severn Valley and the Keighley & Worth Valley, have become famous in their own right. Some of the preserved lines are physically connected to the BR system and one example is the Great Western Society who use the area of the former motive power depot at Didcot. However, except when special trains are run on particular occasions there is rarely any cross-operating with British Rail, mainly for technical or industrial relations reasons.

Beeching realised that railways had to co-exist with other forms of transport, notably road competition for both freight and passengers. But BR in the early 1960s still had a freight system not far changed from Victorian days. Hundreds of stations had small goods yards and coal merchants' sidings even though traffic had dwindled over many years. Beeching swept these away and the yards of suburban stations were converted into convenient car parks to encourage workers to leave their cars safely for the day and take the train to the big city. Now, these car parks are taken for granted, and younger enthusiasts might not even realise there were once freight wagons where cars now stand. Similarly, when the local coal merchants lost their sidings they often retained the land around their coal staithes, bringing in the bulk coal supplies for local distribution by road truck rather than in the coal wagon of old. Thus we have another quite common relic of BR modernisation, the coal merchant near the railway line but no longer physically connected by a spur siding — even though the old coal staithes, office and scales may have stayed just as they were when traffic came by rail. For a very characteristic feature of the modern scene therefore, make a little coal yard divorced from rail contact. The rail-carried coal traffic was meantime transferred to coal concentration

Right:
The original new uniforms for (from left) station inspector, station master and porter in 1965. These styles and additions (new work shirt and blouse) are still to be seen but there are few, if any, model figures readily available in these styles so adaptation of existing figures is necessary.
BR/Ian Allan Library

The new face of British Railways

Behind the many forms in which British Railways appear to the travelling or trading customer stands one national undertaking. So wide is the visible range of activity on today's railways - transport by rail, sea and road, engineering, architecture, catering - that this essential unity tends to become obscured. The new house style, now being introduced, by stages, throughout the system, is an expression in modern terms of this unity. Everything seen and used frequently by the public, every station, every sign, every piece of printed matter, will be given an instantly recognisable family likeness.

This folder has been designed for further use as a wall sheet. Each side expresses different themes. The front explains the role and function of the new house style; the reverse gives a selection of the key activities of the modern railway in the sixties, of which that house style is the expression.

Serving the passenger

Passenger comfort and travelling amenities are the top priorities in the new trains of the sixties. Some, like the Glasgow Blue Trains of the Clydeside electric service, have already proved how well good design pays in terms of greatly-increased revenue within a relatively short time. Another successful new service, the Midland Pullman, has managed to win back passengers from air travel.

Simple, 'unfussy' outlines, brighter colours, more space and light per passenger, a smoother ride in a vehicle that not only looks clean but is easy to keep clean - these are the main elements in modern British train design. It makes full use of the advantages of modern materials and production techniques.

Trains

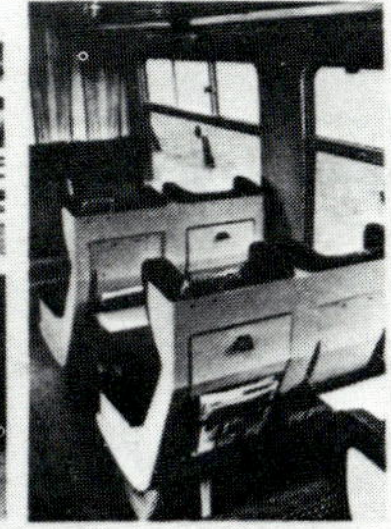

The latest experimental train, XP 64, now on trial, incorporates improved bogies for a better ride, better thermal and acoustic insulation, pressure heating and ventilation, improved toilets, bigger and double-glazed windows, bigger vestibules, better lighting, and wider doors for easy access. The more comfortable seating embodies the results of special research. The thoroughness and detail of the work that went into designing and constructing this train is matched by the detailed market research now being carried out among customers on the train itself.

Stations

A station is far more than a group of buildings where the passenger catches his train, buys a ticket, a meal or a newspaper. It expresses the very nature of rail transport. The new stations, with their functional look, provide for a smooth flow of passengers at all times. Clear signposting, logical arrangement of essential services and spacious interiors match the bold, clean shapes of the external structures. There is the minimum of pretension, the maximum of practical commonsense in architectural terms.

...rporate identity is being extended to the British ...et of over 100 ships. Here, too, the symbol lends ...f continuing purpose in the combination of the ...s of pale grey, blue and flame red. The sea ...is seen to be what it is - an extension of the rail ...

Publicity

Posters on all British Rail Stations will use the new symbol against a background of approved colours. Eye-catching and incisive, it will compel attention from a distance.

The time-table is the most important of all railway publications, the most frequently seen and consulted. It will therefore feature the new symbol boldly on the cover. The symbol instantly identifies the time-table as a British Rail publication; the colour distinguishes one from another.

...nts of the Corporate Identity

British Rail

...ments of the family likeness, or corporate ...y, which can be used and combined in a variety ...s, are:

...w, more purposeful symbol. This replaces the ...lete 'double-sausage' introduced nearly twenty ...s ago.
...dard House Colours intended to replace the ...onal Colours.
...orter name - British Rail - for publicity use and ...on signs.
...stinctive new letter form of thoroughly modern ...gn, for station name-boards, signs, and all ...ted matter.
...w livery for rolling-stock.

Applications

The two-way track symbol lends itself to applications in all kinds of railway settings.

Shown here are: catering, with a table setting in a restaurant car; and the symbol in repetition on a carpet for use in trains and ships. A manual is being prepared to guide everyone in the correct application of the House Style.

Uniforms of more modern cut and style, to be introduced generally, are all part of the new Corporate Identity for British Railways which is now emerging.

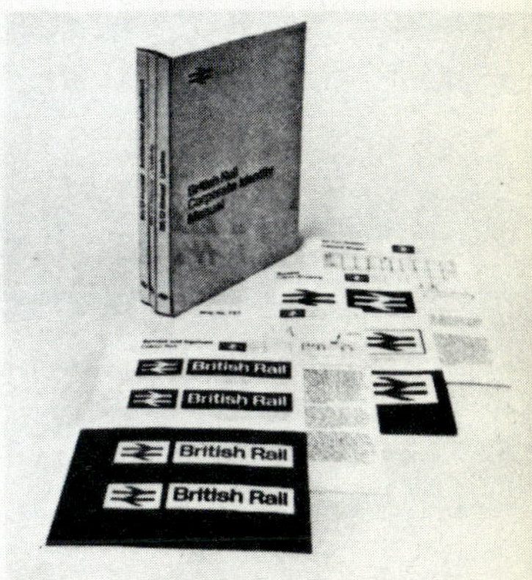

yards, essentially giant versions of the old local coal merchants' sidings, but with advanced handling equipment, which serve many retailers over a large area who now deliver by road from the railhead.

Stations began to change quite radically from the late 1960s and many long hallowed names disappeared completely, for example Bath Green Park (Somerset & Dorset Joint Railway) as the lines it served were closed and abandoned. Closed down stations were often sold as residences, were demolished completely, or were turned into commercial use. Even stations in use were ruthlessly rationalised for simplicity and economy. Typical examples might be the demolition of the station buildings and their replacement with smaller system-built units. Other stations were reduced to unmanned halts or single platform stopping places — and the remaining land, once owned by BR, was sold off.

Surviving branches were often heavily truncated, again with stations much reduced, and track layouts simplified to make them just sufficient for a shuttle service by diesel multiple-unit. At the other end of the scale, some major stations were rebuilt. Euston station became something of a *cause célèbre* when its historic archway was demolished. All this rationalisation has been a continuing programme and it still goes on. The past decade, for example, has seen almost all level crossing gates replaced by lifting barriers, and signalboxes have been much reduced in number by the advent of centralised signalling whereby one box might control a whole route.

This was merely changing an existing system by pruning and improving it, however. Beeching's real master stroke was

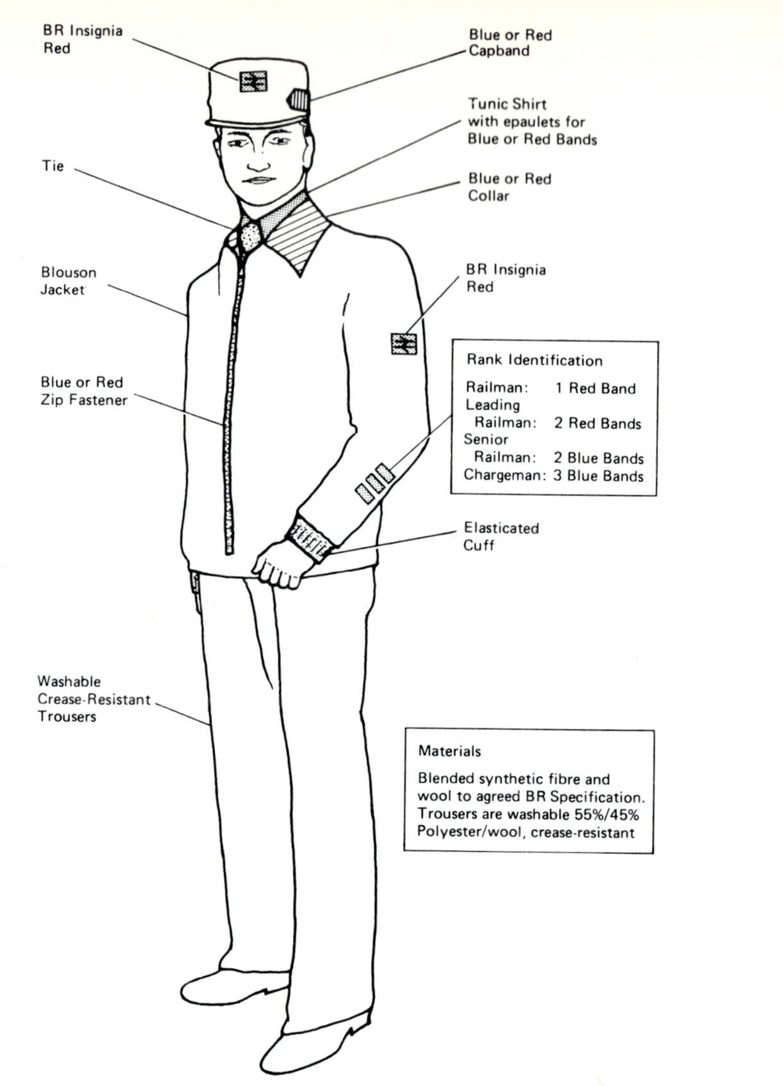

Above left:
Though the original style of BR uniforms are still to be seen, the variation of the 1980s features a very practical blouson with zipper front and blue work shirt. The blouson can be left off in hot weather. This BR diagram shows the style, the details, and the rank markings; no model figures like this were available at the time of writing.
BR/Ian Allan Library

Left:
A classic example of BR rationalisation of a branch terminus. Here is Windermere in 1978 with all but one road of track removed, modern additions to the station and a neglected unused platform and tatty overall roof. This type of simplification would look good duplicated in model form. *John Chalcraft*

Above:
Modern style lifting barrier level crossing at Lolham, near Peterborough. A characteristic feature is the road warning light board and the tall pole carrying a remotely controlled TV camera for safety monitoring. *Chris Cole*

the introduction of a new nation-wide 'corporate image' for the system. It was the new look for the railways, in fact, that caught the public imagination more than anything else and impressed on the customers that British Railways really was changing for the better. Coupled with the new image was a series of technical developments which were intended to keep British Railways in the forefront of passenger train operation, notably in the areas of speed and comfort, which were the main attractions offered by the rival modes of transport — aircraft, cars and coaches.

The existing BR Design Panel was given a strong brief to start from scratch in the provision of new graphics, new colour schemes, new staff uniforms and new interior designs for the next generation of coaching stock. At this time (1963-64), industrial design was very much in the news and with the 'new look' BR there was a golden opportunity to make a clean sweep of the jumble of colours, graphics and designs that then existed. For example, there had been a couple of attempts to produce a BR crest, painting styles for diesel locos were a carry-over from steam locomotives, coach stock colours were either rather dark or drab or a mixture of traditional colours (eg, GWR chocolate and cream), which had resulted from a period when decentralisation had a limited vogue.

First visible evidence of the Design Panel's ideas came with the appearance of the famous XP64 prototype train in May 1964. This made quite an impact. It comprised eight coaches of the proposed Mk 2 design — with wide doorways, bigger windows, new seating styles and an integral body/chassis which gave new coach a pleasing rounded shape. The train was hauled by the latest type of diesel loco then entering service —

the Brush Type 4 (later Class 47). The entire train which included Mk 1 BSKs was painted in the proposed new BR colour scheme and passenger reaction was later put to the test when the set of coaches was used to form one of the 'Talisman' diagrams of those days, hauled by a 'Deltic' class loco, not in the blue livery, but in the two shades of green colour scheme then standard.

The new livery for the coaches was a combination of turquoise blue and pale pearl grey, with bogies and underframes in dark brown. The locomotive was in the same blue with yellow warning panels at the ends and a red patch on each cabside carrying a white double arrow logo type (the red patch was not adopted). After the test period the new colour schemes for stock were finalised and in early 1965 the complete corporate style was announced. It proved to be a most thorough overhaul with a new approach to virtually everything, right down to details like a standard typeface for all lettering, new stationery and literature all in the house style, new staff uniforms, new colours and trading name (Sealink) for BR's shipping fleet, and a new trade name (British Rail) for the railway.

The turquoise blue of the XP64 train was replaced with a slightly darker shade — rail blue. Locomotives were in rail blue and the small yellow warning panels were sensibly extended to take in the full depth of the ends.

Main line coaches were painted in the two-colour blue/pearl grey combination but secondary coaches (and this included locals like DMUs) were painted all blue. However, from 1978 even suburban coaching stock began to appear in the handsome two-tone colour scheme. Freight vehicles initially were given a new data presentation in a neat panel, though later entirely new freight colour schemes were announced. The new uniforms featured a kepi-style cap instead of the old peaked military-style cap, and these initially caused adverse comment — so much did they contrast with the rather scruffy old style uniform. The double arrow logo was also derided at first, 'the arrow of indecision' some called it! On the whole, however, the new look was well received. It did, at last, give a uniform style for BR operations nationwide and it has stood the test of time since 1965 with only minimal adjustments or logical development — for example since 1978 some classes of locomotives have been receiving handsome and striking new livery, a variation of the original style but with grey roof, yellow ends extended round the cab and a giant logo and number. Because of the financial constraints of recent years, however, the repaints only come with major overhauls, so the livery is appearing relatively slowly. Another recent development is in modified uniforms with the introduction of a work shirt and blouse top, plus new grade and/or branch badges and shoulder straps and cap bands in different colours for different branches.

It took some years to get around to repainting and re-signposting all the stations and even in 1984 it was possible to find stations or parts of stations where the original old regional styles could still be found.

On the latest locomotives, Class 58, there is a new Railfreight livery and further livery variations can be expected. There have been local variations also, resulting in locomotives and DMUs with side stripes and so on.

Generally speaking the repainting of locomotives and passenger stock proceeded apace, although there were still a few green locos to be seen as late as 1976, albeit with new number panels for the TOPS renumbering scheme — an innovation of 1971.

TOPS Codes

This is the appropriate time to mention TOPS, not least because it explains the various designations for locomotives and rolling stock. TOPS stands for Total Operations Processing System, a nationwide computer network by means of which BR keeps track of its stock — where it is, where it's heading, where it's standing empty, and so on. The system applies to locomotives and wagons, and in 1983 passenger stock was added to the programme. The idea was adapted from the originator of the idea, Southern Pacific Railroad, USA, and BR have used it since the early 1970s, when locomotives were renumbered to suit the system.

The most noticeable application of the TOPS, however, is to freight stock where codes indicating the type of vehicle replace the long familiar code names which most people used to describe wagons — Toads, Lowmacs, etc. For computer purposes letter groups were necessary and these are carried in the data panel on the vehicle's side, along with its running number and weight indication, etc. The actual allocations of codes is huge, partly because there have been many old wagons in use, and partly because over 10 years or so many new types have come into service and others scrapped. A further complication is that TOPS codes were added only on repainting, so many wagons, even in

Centre right and bottom right:
Newquay station in Cornwall has been partially rebuilt. Outside a row of modern and undistinguished lock-up shops is built across the platform ends, there is a standard BR station sign and logo on a flame red panel, and waiting space for cars. On the platform are modern platform lamps and, beyond the DMU, the old goods yard and carriage siding area has become a large car park. This bit of modernisation is not particularly attractive in its execution. *Richard Gardner*

Above:
The modern station concept is well illustrated by Bristol Parkway, opened in 1972 and situated near the M4/M5 motorway junction. With 'park and ride' appeal in mind it has car parks for over 500 cars. Note simple office block with 'bus shelter' accommodation on platforms and very simple track layout — an ideal prototype for a model station capturing the authentic BR look.
BR/Ian Allan Library

Right:
The BR alphabet and symbol shown in use at Bristol Parkway, and similar to many other new and rebuilt stations throughout the country.
BR/Ian Allan Library

1984 were still running without TOPS code marking.

While TOPS seems complicated the code allocation does use appropriate key letters which help to indicate the vehicle's type and function. The TOPS code is a three letter group of which the first letter indicates vehicle type, the second letter the sub type, and the third the type or brakes. A fourth letter, not painted on the vehicle, indicates a sub-grouping variant.

Some of the letters are self explanatory and an abbreviated list of first letters is as follows:

A   Coaches
B   Bogie steel wagon
CA Brake van
F   Flat wagon
H   Hopper
I   International
M   Mineral wagon
O   Open
P   Private owner
T   Tank wagon
V   Van
W   Container wagon
Y   Departmental vehicle (bogie)

An abbreviated list of third letter (brake indicator) codes is as follows:

A   air brakes
B   air brakes, vacuum pipe
F   vacuum brakes
G   vacuum brakes, air pipe
H   dual brakes (AFI — accelerator freight inshot)
O   hand brake
P   vacuum pipe
R   dual pipe
V   vacuum brake
X   dual brakes

Some common modern types are indicated thus:

HAA — Merry-go-round hopper
  H   Hopper
  A   type A
  A   air brake

VIX — Ferry van
  V   Van
  I   type 1
  X   dual brake (air/vacuum)

CAR — Brake van
  CA Brake van
  R   dual pipe

PWA — Procor 82-tonne pallet van (curtain sides)
  P   Private owner
  W   type W
  A   air brake

YGH — Sealion ballast wagon 40.5 tonne
  Y   Departmental vehicle (bogie)
  G   type G
  H   dual brake

HTV — 21-ton coal hopper
  H   Hopper
  T   type T
  V   vacuum brake

Note that the second letter identifies the precise design of vehicle concerned — indicated above as 'type G' for simplicity, though this has no actual significance. It must also be pointed out that these codes run to hundreds with only random examples given here. Knowing the basic key letters, however, enables the enthusiast to work out the type and braking system of any marked vehicle.

By the use of computer terminals the 'consist' of any train can be quickly transmitted to the yard or other destination and much of the old-fashioned clerical work involved in despatching freight trains is superseded and efficiency is greatly increased.

By 1968 the new look of British Rail was evident everywhere, particularly noticeable to the public in the application of the new colour schemes. The new Mk 2 coaches had entered production from 1964-65, a further development from the XP64 prototypes, and these offered greatly improved comfort with new 'airliner style' interiors. There was another jump forward in comfort and coach design with the superb Mk 3 coaches of the late 1970s. The Mk 3 coach is used in loco-hauled trains on the West Coast main line and they are the standard coaches used in the dramatic InterCity 125 High Speed Trains which entered service in the latter half of the 1970s.

The HST was one of the great British Rail achievements of the 1970s, but a lot more was happening. Great strides were made in electrification of key heavily trafficked routes, a process of modernisation only restrained by lack of investment funds, but impressive, nonetheless, in what was achieved. Among lines electrified earlier were the Glasgow and East of London suburban networks, while the Southern Region had extended electrification to Bournemouth. The West Coast main line was another early route for electrification, a project completed by 1967, though the final stretch to Glasgow was not completed until 1974. The Great Northern (suburban) and the Bedford-St Pancras electrification came later, the latter in 1983.

All this electrification work lead to new stock and locomotives to service the lines, but it should be noted that BR electric trac-tion has not been very well represented by model manufacturers in recent years and only a few items have appeared.

Top:
By contrast, Par in Cornwall has hardly changed since GWR days except for the BR 'rail alphabet' graphics. *Richard Gardner*

Above:
Merit make a kit of the modern signal box shown here (at the manufacturer's local station). The box is now redundant as a result of the new King's Cross control box. *BR/Ian Allan Library*

It must be remembered that change is taking place all the time particularly in respect of colour schemes. For example refurbished DMUs of the late 1970s were attractively painted in white with blue side stripes and brown underframes. This was abandoned after a couple of years and the blue/grey livery (as already used on main line stock) was extended also to DMU sets. But the blue/white sets continued in service, of course, until repainted and could be seen along with standard blue or blue/grey livery in the early 1980s. Also the setting up of regional transportation authorities in the big metropolitan counties led to local markings being added to the standard BR markings, offering yet more variation. A recent change in HST liveries has given them black cab roofs instead of yellow, but the introduction even of this is spread over a long period. More recently a new 'Executive' livery has appeared on HSTs. And so it goes on, but the modern modeller is in the handy position of being able to observe such changes as they happen — take a camera and notebook on your rail journeys.

Typical mixture of old and new at Doncaster in 1980. DMUs in the background are in both 'refurbished' and original all blue livery; there is a train of HAA Merry-go-Round coal hoppers; old vans still in departmental use; Mk 1 and Mk 2 coaching stock; new signalbox and platform extension; old station and works and new structure in the background, with all platform and flood lights in modern style, colour light signals and new station nameboards. The Deltic No 55003 has the livery variation of a white cab roof, applied by Finsbury Park depot unofficially. Note both bullhead and flat bottom track and concrete and wooden sleepers. *John Chalcraft*

3 Motive power survey

For many years, models of current diesel locomotives were remarkably scarce from the major makers of ready-to-run equipment in 4mm scale and N gauge. There were sufficient models to work with but there were great gaps in the range of what was available. Happily, in the past few years the various makers have started to make up for their slow start in this area. Nonetheless, the reluctance on the part of the big manufacturers to get away from 'steam age' models into diesel and electrics was somewhat surprising considering that the customers at the train set end of the market are all too young to have ever seen a steam train except on a preserved line. We had to wait about 13 years after its introduction before any maker brought out an r-t-r model of the important Class 50 in 4mm scale and over 20 years before Lima (a relative newcomer to the British market) brought out a scale length diesel multiple-unit. In the last few years, however, the pace has quickened, as far as motive power is concerned, and there is enough available on the market in 4mm scale to stock the requirements of a layout of virtually any size. There are still gaps, however, in certain areas as we shall see.

A happy development, also, in the last couple of years, has been a fine output of models in N gauge, notably from Graham Farish, and some very good kits in O gauge from David Parkin (locomotives) and Westdale (coaches, DMUs and EMUs) so satisfying the requirements of the three most popular scales. The full extent of what is available always surprises those who have avoided modelling the current scene because of a supposed scarcity of models. In actual fact, there is now almost an embarrassment of riches on the ready-to-run scene alone. Once again, in recent years there has been a pleasing development of detailing and conversion kits which enable ready-to-run models to be super-detailed, varied in their actual fittings, or altered to a similar type. Indeed, a major pleasure with modern era modelling is the sheer volume of simple detailing and conversion which is possible with existing models. This is work well within the capabilities of anyone with basic modelling experience as is demonstrated with some models in the next chapter. All ready-to-run models available are susceptible to the simple detailing work involved, whilst most kits available come with full instructions. In addition, it is often possible to economise on the few pounds cost of a conversion kit, for many simple conversions can be done with scrap metal, plastic card or items from the spares box.

Let's now look at what is available, concentrating only on types in service in the early 1980s.

Diesel-electric and diesel-mechanical locomotives

Diesel-electric locomotives have proved to be rather more durable than most people thought likely when they were first introduced. Many locomotives still in service derive from the original 'pilot scheme' designs of 1955-58 and some classes have indeed outlived later designs. When diesel locos were first put into BR service and up to 1968, they were known by type numbers and their makers' names. Type 1 referred to

machines rated up to 1,000hp, Type 2 to 1,000-1,475hp, Type 3 1,500-1,750hp, Type 4 2,000-2,750, and Type 5 3,000hp or more. What is now a Class 31 was before 1968 known as a Brush Type 2, Brush being the manufacturer. This distinguished it from, say, a BRC&W Type 2 (now Class 27).

This unwieldy and not very precise terminology was replaced by the TOPS scheme in the 1970s, outlined in the last section, which enabled all locomotives to be put on to computer records for traffic and maintenance purposes. For locomotives the class designation was a two-digit group, and the numbers within the class ran from 001-999, so giving a five-figure number group. Thus the Brush Type 2 became Class 31 and a typical locomotive might be 31 146.

We can thus work through the available models class by class.

Class 03

This is a small diesel-mechanical shunter of 204hp. In OO gauge there is a fine model by Mainline depicting a basic loco not fitted with air brakes (which would be an obvious detail modification for the model). There is also a white metal kit by MTK for OO.

Class 04

It is 'cheating' to include this second diesel-mechanical design, for all are now out of BR service. However, if your modelling period is set just a few years ago then an '04' would be legitimate. Also, many were sold for industrial use and are still to be seen. Years ago, there was a good Airfix non-motorised plastic kit — and the body from this fits the Mainline '03' chassis. There is also a complete MTK white metal kit in 4mm scale, and a Langley kit for N gauge. Vulcan have produced a white metal kit for both O and OO gauge versions. A number of '04s' were given 'skirts' round the wheels and motion for dockyard and tramway service (on the Wisbech and Upwell Tramway).

Below:
Mainline's model of the Class 03 diesel shunter is a very good one and is accurately detailed at 4mm scale.

Class 08/09

This is the very familiar standard BR shunter, built in hundreds, descending from an English Electric design for the LMSR and still in very widespread service. The '09' is a version with different gearing and air brakes for the Southern Region only. There is a 4mm model from Wrenn (the old Hornby-Dublo design), a Hornby model, and a Lima model in 4mm scale. Of these, the Hornby model can be discounted as it has an inaccurate chassis. The Wrenn depicts the early production type but it needs the end ladders removed in its modern BR form; and the Lima model is the best of the bunch. It depicts a later production machine and carries an '09' number. It lends itself to simple conversion to EM gauge because of its basic chassis design. Any '08' or '09' model needs detailing to depict a specific machine, however, and details for this are given in the next section. AC Model Engineering produce a cast resin body kit for O gauge.

For N gauge there is a Graham Farish model which has an inaccurate chassis in that it lacks the outside frames. With a little work a purchaser could rectify this omission.

Class 13

This is a 'master and slave' or 'cow and calf' combination of an '08' and a cabless '08' permanently coupled for hump yard work. It can only be achieved by converting two Wrenn or Lima models and is, naturally, an interesting, though challenging project.

Class 20

This was one of the 'pilot series' locos still very much in wide and active service. Today, they are most often used in pairs — cabs outward. A very acceptable model is in the Wrenn range, depicting an early machine with the old headcode discs. It was originally a Dublo release of 1960 and one of the earliest proprietary diesel models. Lima have

Above:

Further detailing is possible even with a good ready-to-run model. All moulded handrails have been replaced with wire, a scale coupler replaces the tension-lock coupler, new screen wipers are fitted and all the small lifting grips on the bonnet sides are fully modelled. Note the blackened tyres and weathered chassis.
Model by Malcolm Carlsson

Right:

Though the Class 04 shunter is no longer in BR service, many are still in industrial use. Here one handles container traffic on Ford's private wharf at Dagenham. *Ford of Britain*

released a model in 4mm scale depicting the later production type. It has all the later detail changes such as headcode boxes and stress-relieving holes in the bogie side frames. For N gauge Graham Farish produce a truly excellent Class 20 which is very accurate and leaves nothing to be desired. For 7mm scale there is a fine kit by Parkin (Postwar Prototypes). The Class 20 is a type of major importance, making it a sound first purchase for any layout in any of the available scales.

Class 25

Hornby produce a very accurate model of the Type 25/1 in 4mm scale — although it does stand a little high on its bogies. The Class 25 model can be altered to other sub-variants using available conversion kits, or by 'do-it-yourself' conversion work. The Class 25/3 is available as a MTK cast metal kit in 4mm scale. For N gauge Graham Farish make a good model.

Class 26/27

These two similar Birmingham Railway Carriage & Wagon types are produced as white metal kits in 4mm scale by MTK, but it is easier to convert the Lima Class 33 r-t-r model using Westward conversion kits or a 'do-it-yourself' job as described in the next section. Hornby-Minitrix produce a representation of a Class 27 for N gauge, but it uses a German chassis and is far from accurate, though an exceptionally good performer.

Class 31

The original Brush Type 2, this old warhorse is still going strong. Over the years, their ranks have thinned out and there are several sub-variants. Some years ago there was a Hornby Class 31 for the OO gauge, but the Airfix model was the definitive replica in recent years (whether Mainline, who acquired Airfix, will again produce the model is a matter of conjecture). Lima makes a N gauge version but this is overscale and not really to be commended.

Class 33

This Southern Region workhorse, in service since 1962, is available as a Class 33/1 kit by MTK or r-t-r as a Class 31/0 by Lima. This Lima model is a good one, needing only basic detailing. They have also produced an O gauge version needing new accurate bogie side frames (available in the Ascott range) and extra details. Some years back they produced an HO version which can still occasionally be found on the secondhand market, but it should be noted that this 1:87 scale HO model will not mix with the newer 1:76 scale OO models.

Class 37

This highly important type, and another old workhorse still going strong in the 1980s, has long been available from Hornby. Though the body moulding is good and it captures the character of the original, the chassis and running gear is inaccurate demanding a fair amount of work to produce a good model. For N gauge, there is a good model from Graham Farish, but as this uses a modified Class 47 chassis it is not wholly correct. However, it can be greatly improved by removing the incorrect cab steps from the bogies (intended for the Class 47) and adding new ones lined up with the Class 37 door. In O gauge there is a good Parkin (Postwar Prototypes) kit for a Class 37.

Class 40

Jouef produced a 4mm scale ready-to-run model — although it is only available on the secondhand market, as it is no longer in current production. The model is basically good and needs only a little extra detailing. There is also a MTK kit in 4mm scale, and Parkin produce a kit for O gauge.

Class 45/46

Mainline make a basically sound model of the Class 45 which with detail changes will also depict a Class 46. The Mainline model has been produced in several forms including early and late nose fittings. Again detail improvements are needed to make the model fully accurate in detail. An excellent Class 45/46 kit for 7mm scale is produced in the Parkin range.

Below:
Hornby's Class 25/3 is a very good model, even as taken out of the box, but it can be improved with further detailing .

Above left:
Class 31 has been widely used all over BR except the Southern Region. Here is seen No 31251 at Great Shelfold on a Cambridge-Liverpool Street train in July 1976. At that time the four-digit headcodes had recently been abandoned and the codes set to 0000 pending alteration to marker lights as now used. Note typical East Anglian scene with grain mills and light industry flanking the tracks. *John M. Capes*

Above:
Widely used on the Southern Region for over 20 years is the popular Class 33 'Crompton' locos. Here is No 33039 running round its train at Exeter St Davids in the time-honoured way, prior to working the return leg of its roster to Waterloo. Note mini snowploughs and old style lamp-irons. Headcode (two digit) in Southern Region style is carried in the centre panel with red squares (seen here) displayed at the opposite (rear) end. Old style signal gantry remains in use here, but is not likely to remain for long. The Class 50s are now rostered on this route. *John Chalcraft*

Centre left:
The Mainline Class 45 is a fine 4mm scale model. As supplied, however, it has various details which need amending including removal of the prominent gutter line at roof edge and plating over of the side body steps and (in some locos) plating over of water filler apertures.

Bottom left:
This view of No 45006 at Temple Meads shows key detail changes. Note the plated over body side climbing rungs, plated over roof apertures and nose modified to show marker lights only.
John Chalcraft

Left:
The Mainline model of the Class 45 is an easy one to convert to EM gauge, mainly just by opening the wheels on the axles using the EM Gauge Society's back-to-back gauge.

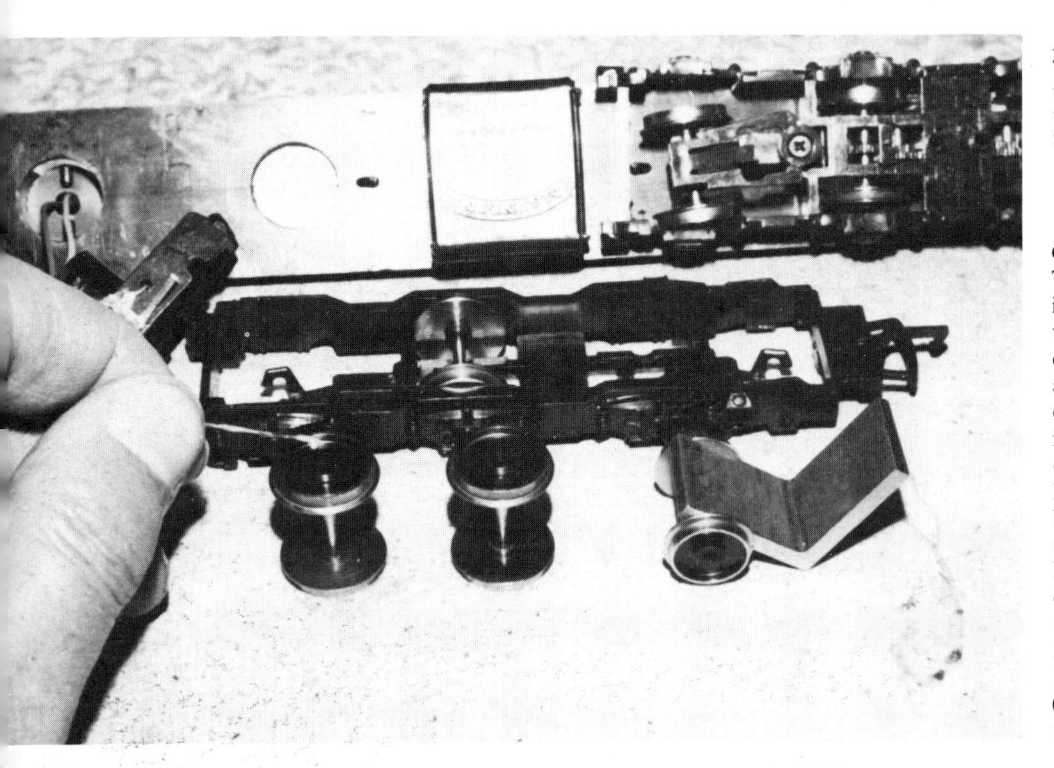

Class 47

This is the modern universal locomotive and it is much modelled. The Hornby 4mm scale version is an old one leaving much to be desired in the way of improvements — a fair amount of work is necessary to get a well detailed model, although the basic model in its latest form, does, in fact, capture the character well. MTK produce a 4mm scale kit and for N gauge there is a very fine model by Graham Farish in several colour schemes. Hornby-Minitrix also produce a N gauge model of high quality — though it does have the early type roof shutters which are appropriate only to the 1964-68 period. For 7mm scale there is a fine kit, again by Parkin, which makes up well. In Z gauge (1:220) there was a model by Ellmar Products using a Mârklin chassis.

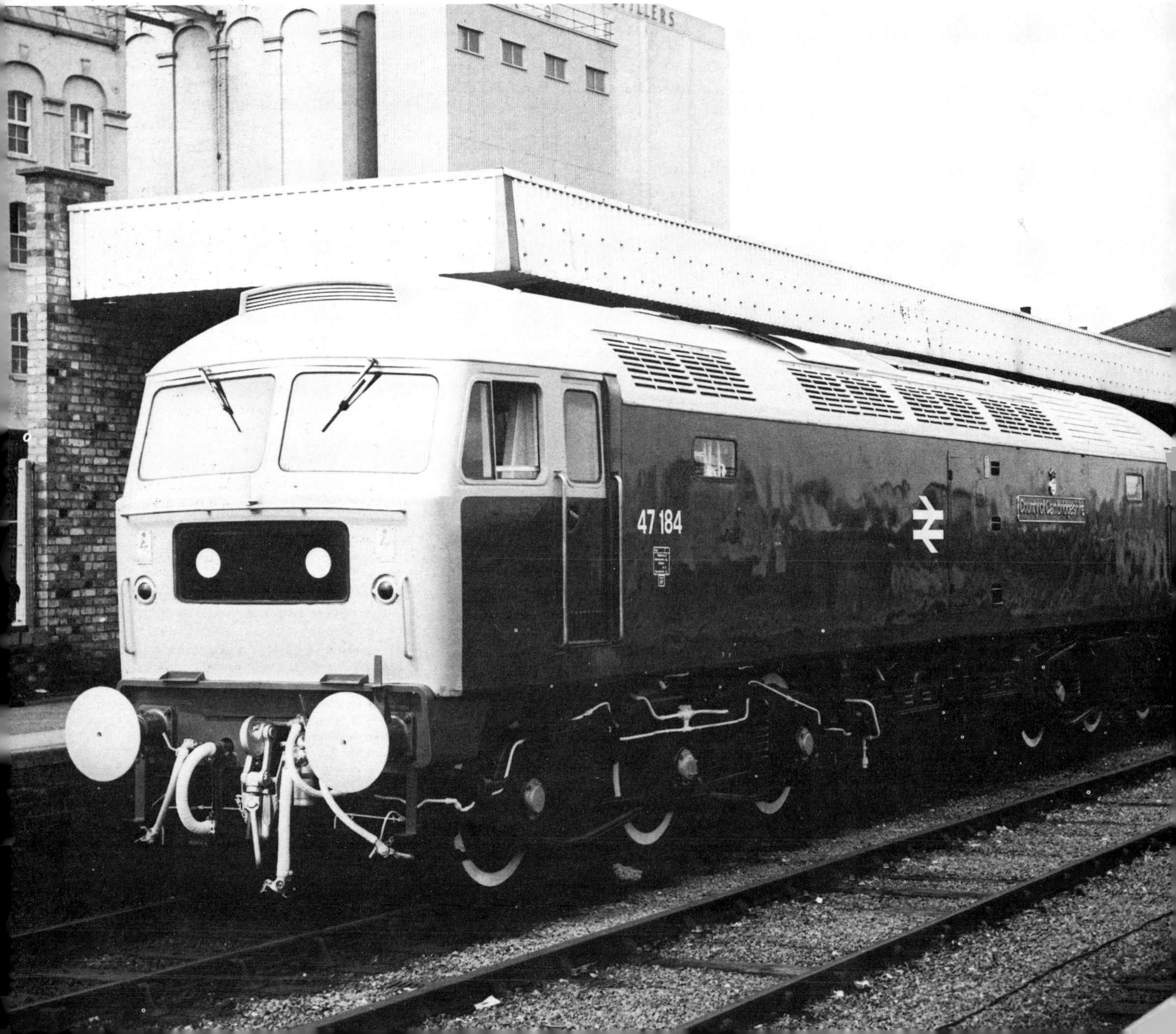

Class 50

A good Lima model is available for 4mm scale, depicting the original style. It is also available in kit form for 4mm scale from MTK, Jidenco and Q Kits. Extra work is required to convert these models to the latest refurbished Class 50 appearance. (See next section.)

Class 55

This is the famous 'Deltic', the 'greyhounds' of the East Coast route before their withdrawal in early 1982. Though no longer in service they will appeal to any modeller of the recent past and are classics of their kind. The Lima model is accurate except for slight shortening of the noses and the bogie wheelbase — not noticeable. Minor detailing will enhance the model. There is a N gauge model by Lima but it is modelled overscale.

Class 56

The most recent of the BR production batches, the big Class 56 type is seen on unit and 'merry-go-round' trains. Mainline released a good model in 4mm scale in r-t-r form and MTK and Q Kits produce kits in this scale. In 7mm scale there is a complete kit by Parkin.

Class 58

The very latest type entering service, this radically different looking machine is styled to appeal to export markets and has a boxy looking, 'hood' type body. Hornby released a good model in 1983 ahead of the actual prototype. When the new loco appeared, detailed changes to fittings and colour schemes had been made, necessitating minor changes on the Hornby model, as shown in the picture.

Left:
Several Class 47s have been handsomely painted and named. Here is No 47184 *County of Cambridgeshire* **after being named in May 1979. The roof is pearl grey, buffers, pipes and piping is white.** *John M. Capes*

Top:
Extra detail for the Lima model of the Deltic. Horns, screen wipers, marker light box and grab rails and buffer beam fittings are being added, all typical additions for a ready-to-run model.

Above:
Hornby produced a smart model of the Class 58 before the real locomotive had actually appeared. This caused problems because BR made detail changes (seen in the next illustration) while completing the loco. *Hornby Hobbies*

Right:
The actual Class 58 shown on the day it left the assembly shop at Doncaster Works in December 1982. *Colin J. Marsden*

Obsolete Locomotives

In addition to the current types listed, there are a number of others which would qualify for a layout depicting the scene a few years ago, though they are no longer currently in service.

Class 21/29

This old favourite was one of the 'pilot scheme' types which was relatively unsuccessful. These suffered from unreliability and a new engine was fitted to most (changing them from Class 21 to 29). All were scrapped by the early 1970s (having by then all been transferred to the Scottish region). A good model in 4mm scale is produced by Hornby — one of their best. Some extra detailing is needed.

Class 24

These were predecessors of the Class 25 and were similar in appearance. By 1981 they were all withdrawn. There is a MTK kit for 4mm scale and a Langley body line kit for N scale.

Class 35

These were the famous 'Hymeks', diesel-hydraulics of the Western Region and were withdrawn in the 1970s. There is a good Hornby model in 4mm scale, a Peco body line cast kit (to fit an Arnold chassis) in N, and a Novo (ex-Hornby) battery model in O gauge. This is out of production, but is a cheap starter for 7mm scale, if one can be obtained.

Class 42/43

The famous 'Warship' class of diesel-hydraulic locos were everybodys favourite although withdrawn in the 1970s having worked on the Western and Southern Regions. Their names were subsequently allocated to the Class 50 locos.

In 4mm scale there are models by Mainline and Lima, the former being a superb model and one of the best of all ready-to-run models. There is also a magnificent model in HO gauge (3.5mm scale) from Fleischmann. Hornby-Minitrix produce a model for N scale although the body is a little oversize for correct scale.

Class 52

This was the 'Western' class, another Western Region diesel-hydraulic withdrawn in the 1970s. There are r-t-r models by Lima and Hornby in 4mm scale, both good, while MTK and Q Kits made kit versions. There is a 7mm kit by Parkin.

As a matter of history the diesel-hydraulics of the Western Region were withdrawn before the end of their normal life span because BR decided to standardise on diesel-electrics only. The diesel-hydraulics required more expensive maintenance. Now all BR locos are diesel-electrics — except for a few small diesel-mechanical shunters.

Obviously the models noted as kits in the foregoing lists may not be suitable for beginners or less experienced workers. In many cases (eg, Parkin) they come as body kits only and suitable motors and bogies have to be purchased separately.

Diesel Multiple Units

If the market is rich for the diesel loco enthusiast, the same cannot be said for the ubiquitous DMUs. In the model field they were for years conspicuous by their absence despite the fact that full-size diesel multiple-units are seen in almost every part of the country. Tri-ang (in their pre-Hornby days) produced a Metro-Cammell set which falls below today's standards and is now out of production. Trix produced a Trans-Pennine DMU (to 1:80 scale) but this is also out of production. In recent years, however, Lima have produced a Class 117 set for 4mm scale available in three relevant colour schemes — blue, blue/grey, and the refurbished blue/white scheme. This set needs extra detailing and the driving trailer requires major work on it to eliminate the unwanted guard's compartment — for as a production economy Lima made only a motor brake second body and duplicated it in unmotorised form.

Hornby more recently produced a Class 110 DMU in 4mm scale, and this is a superb

Lima's model of the Class 117 DMU is generally accurate save for the lack of steps and other small details from the chassis. To be fully accurate, however, the unpowered motor brake second must be converted to a motor second. The guard's compartment is cut away and another unpowered motor brake second is cut up and the segments are rearranged as in the second illustration to give a correct motor second. The small segment is turned back to front to get the window bays in the correct order.

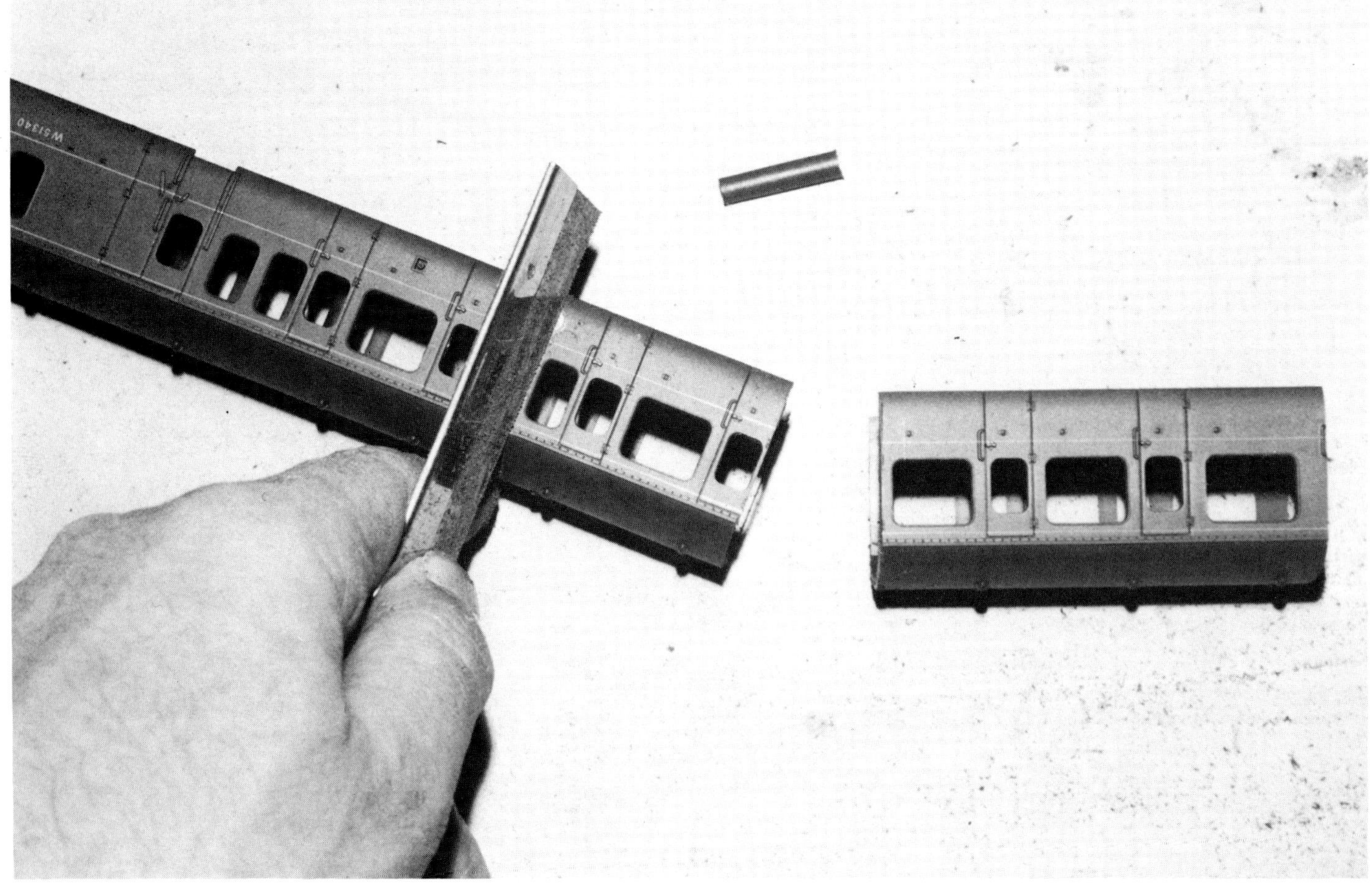

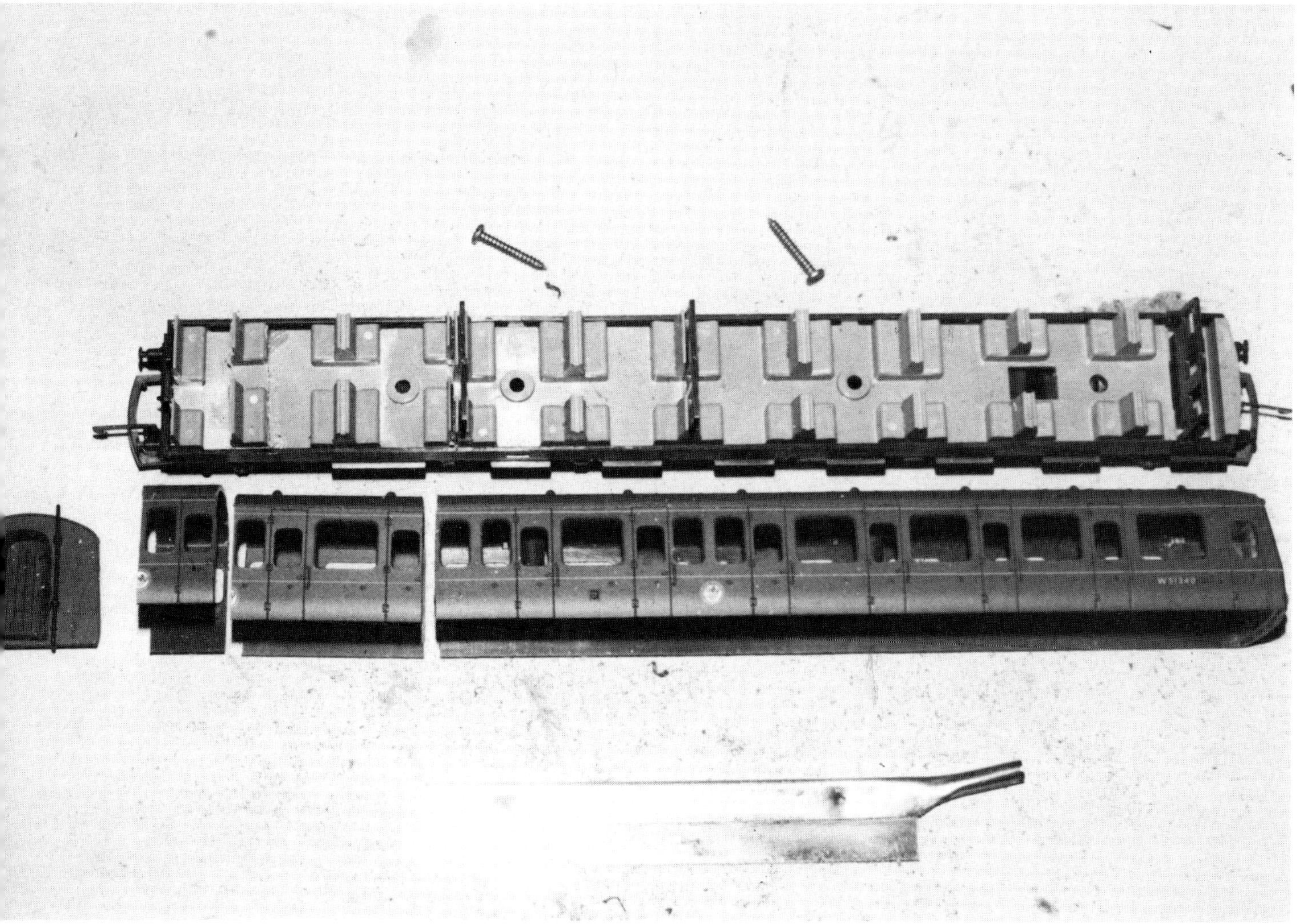

Left:
Here is the result — the motor second coupled to the motor brake second.

Below left:
A useful tip for close-coupling of DMUs and EMUs or coach sets or rakes, without buffer locking is to use the Roco HO scale close-coupler in place of the ugly tension lock type.

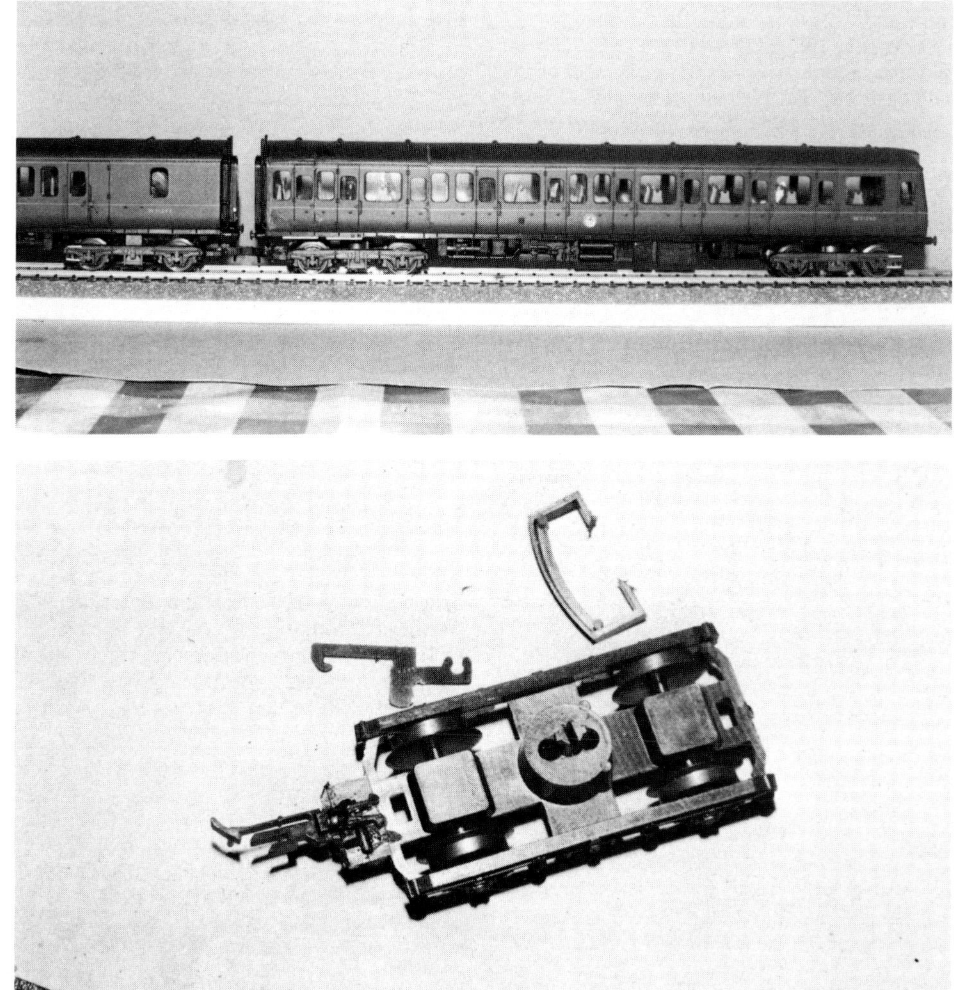

model, one of the firm's best even as it comes. It has excellent performance and is available in the blue/white 'refurbished' livery. The real units, however, operate only in the North of England. Both models of the Class 110 and 117 dmus have conversion potential to other units.

There are no other ready-to-run DMUs in 4mm scale though there are several kits in the MTK range. The only equipment in N scale is an excellent Metro-Cammell Class 101 by Graham Farish which comes in blue, or blue/grey for the modern era.

Finally in this category is the High Speed Train, BR's principal InterCity express type. Hornby were the first in the field with this in 4mm scale and their power cars depict the original appearance of the early HSTs and are to scale size. They also produce the Mk 3 coaches to make up a complete HST train, but these are short on scale length by the omission of one seating bay or its equivalent. This makes for less extreme overhang on tight curves in a train set and there is some merit in this 'shortie' approach. The more

Above:
The Hornby OO gauge model of the Class 86 is a fine runner and a good looker.

modern releases however, by Lima, provides full length scale coaches and the power cars depict the later production type with exhaust smoke deflector on the roof and the guard's compartment deleted, thus a full length HST can be obtained straight from the manufacturer's boxes.

For N scale there is a fine HST set by Graham Farish who provide the necessary coaches to make up an excellent replica of the train.

Electric Locomotives

Again, there is a surprising shortage of modern electric locomotives in any scale. But in recent years Lima have produced a 4mm scale model of Class 87 and Hornby have a Class 86 in the same scale. These are both very good models, not only in appearance but also in performance.

Formerly available were a Class 76 from Hornby and a Class 81 from both Hornby and Liliput. In N scale there is a Lima Class 81 and Lima also have plans for a Class 87 in the smaller scale. In addition to these, MTK produce 4mm scale kits of Southern Region electro-diesels of Classes 73 and 74 (the latter no longer in BR service).

Regarding ordinary electric multiple-units there are none in ready-to-run form and just a few SR types in kit form from MTK, so except for scratch building it is difficult for anyone to model modern EMUs.

The Advanced Passenger Train, the supreme EMU, is available from Hornby but in this case the manufacturer produced a model of the prototype ahead of the completion of BR's testing programme when many failures occurred. At the time of writing, the APT is being withdrawn and will be heavily revised. Before it is again tested. If, and when, it re-appears it is bound to be entirely different from the original design; thus, unfortunately, Hornby's model will be unprototypical.

Catenary

For a Southern Region layout using MTK kits, a dummy outside third rail is really all that is required for 100% realism, but everywhere else an overhead wire pick-up system is necessary for complete authenticity. Several Continental manufacturers make complete systems which can be obtained in this country and Sommerfeldt, JV, Lima, Vollmer and Piko all make model catenary which will be suitable, although not necessarily accurate to BR practice. The JV parts are remarkably similar to the BR style and is the best from the point of view of the prototypical appearance. This can be obtained from Hadley Hobbies of London.

Left:
While overhead catenary equipment may be purchased, here it is scratch-built and beautifully made to suit the site by Peter Shaw of Southport.
Brian Monaghan

4 Improving the breed

Some Practical Examples

In a small book like this there is not space for completely exhaustive instructions for the conversion and/or detailing of every available modern locomotive. In any case, the model railway magazines quite frequently carry articles on the specific projects and new models are always coming along and tend to get covered by articles soon after they appear. For the benefit of complete beginners, however, or those coming anew to the idea of modelling modern BR through reading this book, here are some actual examples of fairly simple conversion or detailing projects to get you started. It is important to emphasise how vital it is to study the prototype either through photographs, book illustrations, or observation of the real thing — for there is much variation in detail within any loco class. It is easy enough to get the numbers wrong, specific details wrong, or omit key fittings simply by lack of study of the subject. It is sound advice to decide which specific loco you will produce *before* you begin and not worry about it after the model is finished.

In the examples here, Class 50 No 50.001 *Dreadnought* was decided on from the start and hence the Lima model with the old colour scheme was purchased as at the time the model was detailed (1983) this particular loco was in the old colour scheme. It would have been inaccurate to have converted and named this loco in the 'new' livery which *Dreadnought* did not carry.

Naturally there are no short cuts if you build from kits, and the various kits mentioned here need care and reasonable skill to complete — though the Parkin (Postwar Developments) loco kits and Westdale coach kits in 7mm scale are easier than most.

But it is the many ready-to-run models now available in 4mm and N scales that makes modelling the modern scene very attractive to the enthusiast who may never have scratch-built or have kit building skills. Not that the skills are great, but it sometimes takes courage to start. These modern models tend to be recent 'state-of-the-art' releases of great excellence — such as the Lima HST or the Hornby Class 110 DMU. Most are superb models as they come but for production and economic reasons they almost always omit small details. This is where the modeller with limited time or skill can score. It takes only a few hours' work in most cases to transform a good but basic ready-to-run locomotive into a well detailed showpiece.

Several small firms who are specialists now offer detailing or conversion kits of cast or etched pieces for specific models. In essence, you just buy the kit, add the bits and pieces to your purchased model, and touch up the paintwork to fit. Westward, M&L, Craftsman, Crownline, Jackson-Evans and Chris Leigh are among small firms producing this type of kit. They make the going relatively easy for any modeller, especially beginners. And adding the extra detail certainly transforms any modern loco or DMU and makes the hobby much more satisfying than merely running models straight out-of-the-box.

Therefore, if you start modelling the modern era do have a go at improving or detailing a locomotive — this certainly adds a new dimension to the hobby. This applies mainly to 4mm scale where the scope is greatest. For N scale most locomotive models, notably those by Graham Farish, are pleasingly accurate and the large N scale coupler effectively prevents addition of brake and MU pipes, etc, even if they were noticeable in this tiny scale; unless, of course, it is deliberately removed from one end.

If you are running to a tight budget, it is worth pointing out that quite a few conversions can be done using nothing more than basic materials — paper or plastic card for new panelling, Bambi staples or wire for handrails or lamp brackets, plastic scrap for such items as brake cylinders, plastic covered bell wire for air brake hoses, steam heat hoses, multiple-unit connections and guitar G string for vacuum pipes. (One G string from a music shop will last you a long time!) These items apart, you'll need the usual basic tools consisting of craft knife, fine file, razor saw, small screwdrivers (for dismantling work), pin drill and so on. For the newcomer to the model railway hobby, detailing and improving basic locomotives is an interesting introduction to the art of railway modelling.

At this point also, it should be mentioned that anyone who prefers to work in the correct EM gauge for 4mm scale (ie 18.2mm instead of the 16.5mm gauge of OO) will find modern locos and stock the easiest of all to convert. Examples of EM conversion are shown here as an extra option. These methods make simple use of existing wheels, by opening them out on the axles. Nearly all Hornby and Lima models can be altered easily by this method. Wagons and coaches merely have their wheelsets replaced using the appropriate wheelsets for EM made and advertised by such firms as Wheelrights, Ultrascale and Kean-Maygib. In fact, EM is ridiculously easy with diesel and electric locomotives, even if you found steam locos difficult to convert.

Below:
The reason why you need to choose your prototype before proceeding with detailing or converting. Nos 08459 and 08734 were both Doncaster Works shunters in July 1981, yet they differed in number styles, placement of the BR logo and one has a panelled door, one a steel door. No 08459 also has tall vertical front handrails not present on the other loco. It has a black buffer beam while the other has a yellow one. Finally note that No 08459 has four electric headcode lights while No 08734 has only two, a recent reduction seen on some of the Class 08s.
O. H. S. Owen

Right:
For the EM conversion you will need a spare driven wheelset. Take this apart and use a razor-saw to cut the gear wheel very carefully from the hub. It is essential to cut flush to get the full thickness of the gear wheel.

The Class 08 diesel shunter needs even more care, for the hundreds of these machines in service exhibit much variation in the way they are fitted out — wood doors, steel doors, different lockers, and/or different hand rails, are all points to look for. The answer is to find an actual loco with the features of the model (or the features you choose to alter) and give the model that number.

Class 08 Diesel Shunter (Lima)

This is an inexpensive but good model lacking in some details. There is a fairly simple way of converting it to EM gauge by using a second drive gear cut from a spare wheelset (available as a spare item). However, the EM side of things is optional. This model depicts a specific loco and serves also to include a demonstration of how to achieve the flat powdery finish found on real locos in need of repaint. The model is from the Lima range and would make a pleasing first loco for a modern era layout. Follow the picture panel for the actual work involved.

Above left:
Now unscrew the baseplate from the chassis, so releasing the wheels. Keeping handling to a minimum, use a small screwdriver and/or finger pressure to ease each wheel out on its axle by an equal amount to achieve the 18.2m gauge of EM. Use the EMGS back-to-back gauge to do an accurate job. Unscrew the crank nuts on the rear (driven) wheels only and release these completely.

Above:
Take off the geared driving wheel from the rear axle and use a pin to apply a contact adhesive or Super Glue, following the maker's instructions for application. Add the second gear disc to the integral wheel disc and leave the glue to dry out very thoroughly.

Above:
When the glue is set, reassemble the wheel to the axle, using the EMGS back-to-back gauge again to achieve the correct wheel spacing.

Above right:
Put the screws back into the baseplate. Ensure the motor gears mesh with the double-thickness gear wheel. Then test the chassis with ballast weight in place on EM track and through EM turn-outs. All should run well, just like the original OO model, but if adjustments are necessary make them now.

Centre right:
Return the axle to its slot, ensure the wheels and coupling rods are correctly lined up, then put the cranks back on the hubs and secure the original nuts which hold them in place. This underside view clearly shows the double thickness gear wheel on the driven wheel which will ensure the widened wheelset still meshes with the motor gearing.

Bottom right:
Last job on the chassis is to add the missing sandpipes from lengths of thin Microrod bent to shape. If you are not requiring the EM version, start your work on the model at this stage, leaving the chassis and wheelsets as they come.

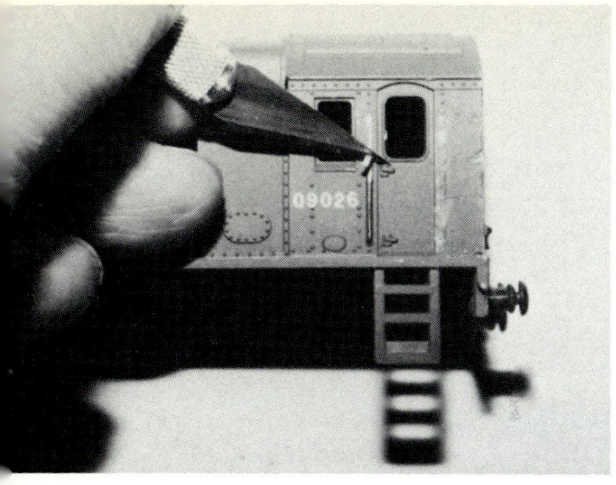

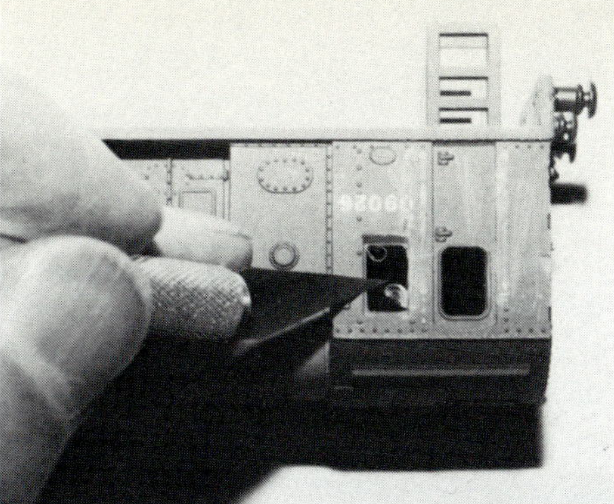

Keep the body separate from the chassis. Use a sharp knife and file to remove the moulded handrails from cab and hood side.

Left:
Though you could fit flush window glazing if required, in practice the glazing looks good enough if simply cemented behind the cab windows. The side windows are definitely too small, however, but are much improved if you cut away the moulded framing within the window area.

Right:
Here we see all the basic detail added to the body shell, though there was variation on some locos. For example many have the locker missing near the cab. On the Lima model this can be sawn away and the gap can be filled with plastic card and the section detailed to match the other side. However, it is easier to select a prototype machine which has this locker fitted. Shown here are cab handrails from No 56 staples adjusted for length with pliers, side handrail from wire, and end step and hood vertical handrails, again from No 56 office staples. Also added is a centre-line 'spine' from plastic card strip on the hood top, runners for the cab roof hatch (file off the rivets from this hatch, also). Finally note the dropped light in the cab side — it is glazed only at the bottom with a strip of plastic card as the top frame.

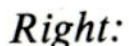

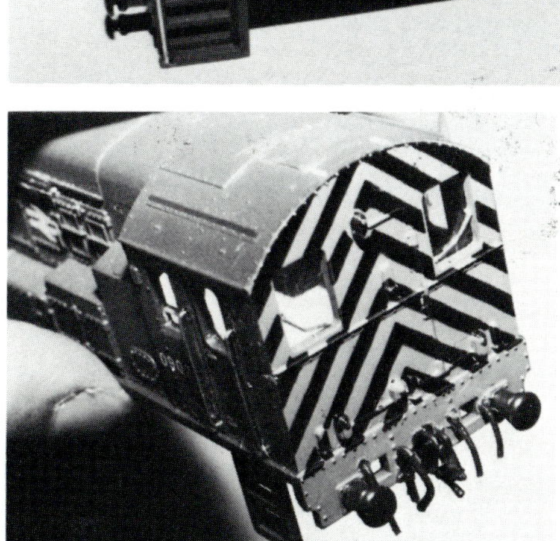

At the front end add either a dummy coupler or a working scale coupler if you are not using tension-locks. Then add the various air brake, vacuum brake, MU connections, etc, using either cast parts or bell wire, guitar string, etc, to suit.

Left:
Rear end shows glazed cab windows, dummy screw coupler from Airfix brake van kit, hose connections, and screen wipers made from lengths of Bambi staple bent to shape and glued to window glazing. New cab handrails can be seen here, also.

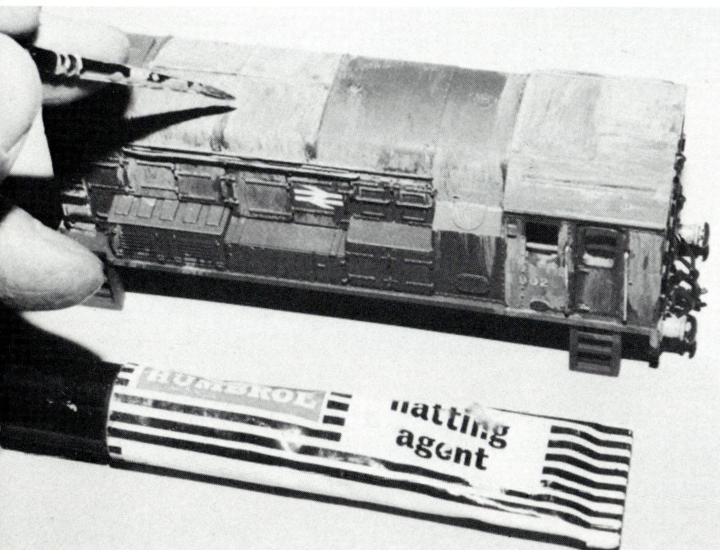

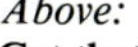

Above:
Get that powdery faded finish by overpainting panels with Humbrol BR blue to which excess Humbrol flatting agent is added.

Above:
The completed model of No 08844 marked with warning panels, stencils etc, matching the actual loco, and with the faded finish of a loco that is soon due for repainting.

Class 50

The Lima model is a good one but depicts the original appearance. It is very easy to add the features related to the 'refurbished' version of the loco. For the beginner it is another simple one for the first attempt.

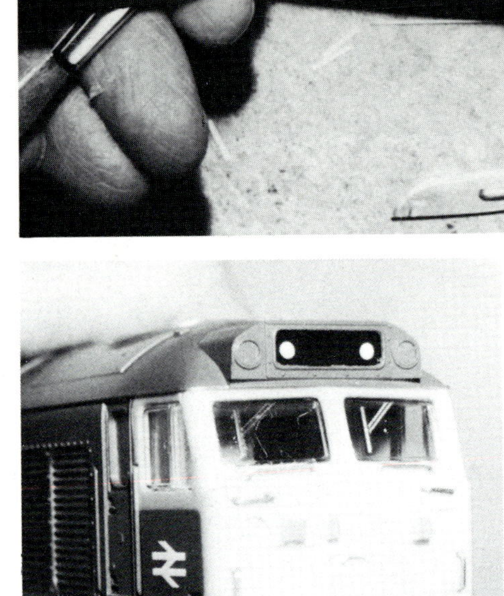

Right:
Start by cutting a stiff paper panel dimensioned to fit the roof cut-out section. Cement it in place (right). At the opposite end fill in the engine room window aperture with lengths of Microstrip stuck in layers to give a grille effect, as is being done here. Repeat on other side.

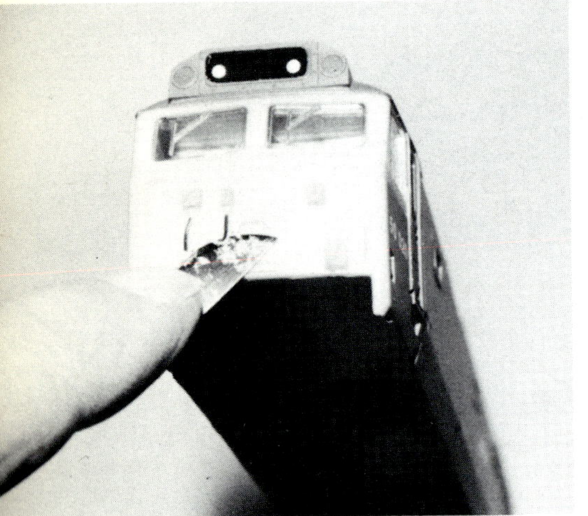

Far left:
With a sharp craft knife carefully carve off the moulded cable and handrail ridges from each end.

Left:
Though the windscreen lower edges should slope slightly more downwards and out, when Bambi staples replaced the ugly moulded handrails beneath the screen the whole appearance improved without the need to enlarge the windows. The smaller horizontal and vertical rails were bent from wire using pliers, all inserted and glued into pre-drilled holes. Roco driver figures were added in cabs.

Right:
On the bogies make up cab steps, either from Microstrip or from thick plastic signal laddering (left over from kits), as here. Add small platforms from plastic cards above the buffer shanks with 6mm lengths of N gauge signal laddering as steps. Remove the coupler hook (unless scale couplers are being fitted) and add Crownline brake pipes and a jumper cable from wire.

Right:
Now seal up the end sandbox filler apertures either with Milliput sanded smooth, or with rectangles of plastic card, but to fit flush. Add a small disc (a computer tape punching is ideal) to depict a plated over gauge adjacent to the second sandbox filler gap. Cut lifting/jacking eyes (for each side) from 20thou plastic card, and cement them to the moulded strongbacks on the lower body edge. Finally cut elongated eyes for the bogie securing chains and cement them to the recess just behind and below the doors. This is just being done in this view. Repeat this work each side.

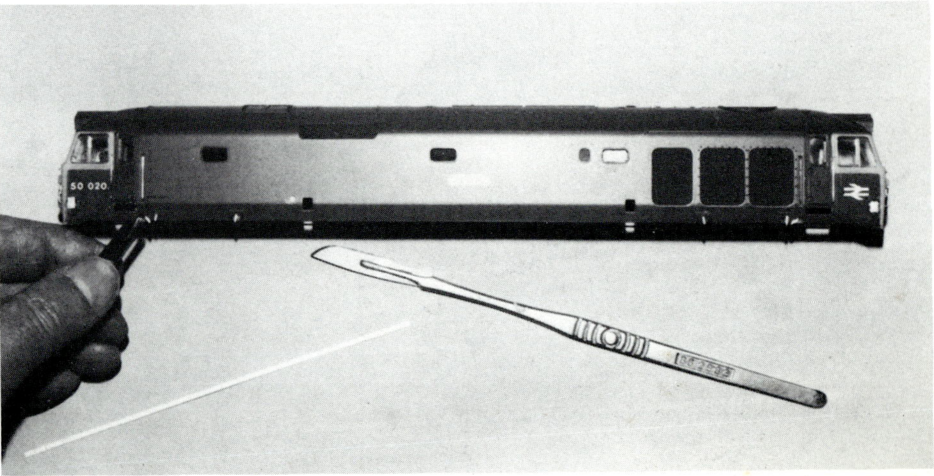

Above:
Here is the completed model before the amended details are painted. All additions show in white. Note slow speed control box added to centre axle box and guard irons on bogie ends, from plastic strip. The central headlight can be cut from a 3mm diameter card punching with a disc of clear plastic for a glass. Just visible here, above the vertical nose handrails, are lamp irons, made from 3mm lengths of Microstrip. The new jumper cable is from bell wire.

Right:
Model after painting and light weathering shows driver in cab, overhead warning signs added, and number amended from Kingprint Letraset BR sheet — plus addition of data panel. CGW nameplate for *Dreadnought* is cemented over original name.

Right:
This view of the modified roof shows the large new panel over the original cut-away section, and next to it a new paper panel stuck over the panel framing which the model carries at this point. Most important is the complete removal of the centre walkway framing (arrowed section) which is carved away before painting the roof.

Class 31 (Airfix/Mainline)

The Airfix/Mainline Class 31 is a highly accurate replica of the real thing and is a good workaday model. It can be converted to EM gauge by filing slightly on the inside of the bogie sideframes and easing out the wheels equally on all axles until the EMGS back-to-back gauge indicates the correct setting for the 18.2mm gauge (back-to-back is actually 16.5mm for EM).

Only minor detail work is required for this model and the chance was taken to add one of the unofficial adornments seen in recent years — a white stripe down the sides. The loco, No 31.411, occasionally worked as a loco for the Royal Train (for which it was highly polished) but the model is depicted as the loco appeared in its role as a station pilot at King's Cross. This model is actually a Class 33/4.

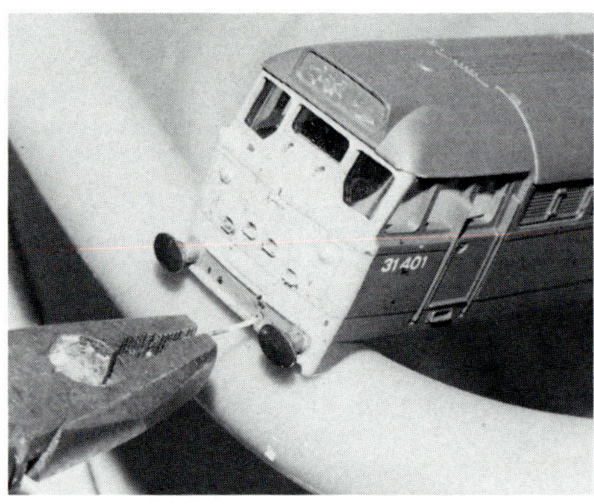

Right:

The handrail on the nose and the various pipes and connections on the buffer beam can all be added to bring the model an attractive degree of detail. You can drill out holes for all these with a Minidrill, but if you don't own one of these a quick way of making the holes is with a hot pin held in pliers. This is how to do it but take great care: hold the model firmly with your free hand, and mark out the hole positions very precisely before you begin (this method is not commended for unsupervised youngsters as hot pins and gas rings can cause injury if care is not taken). It is a matter of moments to pierce out the holes at each end. Clean off any resulting stringing or ridges round the holes using a sharp knife.

Above:

Remove the body from the chassis, and set the latter to one side. As the Class 31/4 has its steam boiler out of use, the side steps to the filler cap on the roof are sealed off with strips of ordinary white writing paper glued with polystyrene cement applied very thinly. Cut the strips 5mm wide, and the sheeting on the roof just marginally bigger

than the apertures to be covered. The bars inside the side windows are most easily made from the thinnest slivers of Microstrip, though wire could be used. Paint the strip matt grey first and this gives quite a realistic metal effect when seen through the glazing. The strips were held in place by small blobs of Uhu on the glazing strip between the window openings.

Above right:

It now remains to add the small missing details. Prominent on each nose is the horizontal handrail now seen in place above the door housing, and an 'ear' on each side which is actually a cover for screen washing nozzles. Pieces of thick (40thou) plastic card, 3mm long and 1.5mm wide, are cut for these. Scrape off the paint and glue them in place at 45deg.

Left:

Bambi staples are exactly right for the top nose handrail — just add a touch of plastic cement and drop it into the holes. Use a staple to mark the exact hole position before you drill or burn the holes. Guitar G string is used for the brake and heat pipes each side of the coupler position.

Ordinary plastic-covered bell wire is fine for the long MU connection coming from the upper edge of the buffer beam while 30amp fuse wire can be used for the electrical connections, curved and stuck under the front corners of the skirting. The last extra fitting, applicable to Class 31/4 only, is the connection box and cable for the electric train heating. A 2.5mm square scrap of thick plastic card depicts the box just above the right-hand buffer (viewed from head on), while a longer length of 30amp fuse wire acts as the cable and is popped into a hole drilled just below the box. The other end is cemented under the front skirt. Lastly add screen wipers easily made by cutting Bambi staples in half and bending them to shape. They can be cemented on to the screen or into holes drilled at the screen edges.

Right:

Because the blue plastic is well done on the Airfix Class 31 you only need blue paint to touch up the modifications. The yellow noses need completely repainting. The area painted red on the model's buffer beam, and indeed all below this level, should be painted black. The white stripe, carried by a few locomotives, is certainly a natty addition. Use Kemco striping for this as it has no unsightly carrier film and can be applied straight from the sheet. Paint out the '0' from the number and replace it with a transfer '1' in the running number. The warning signs and new BR symbol are from the King's Cross dry transfer set.

Class 26 (Lima conversion)

Here is a more complicated conversion which actually produces a type not available in ready-to-run form. Starting with the Lima Class 33, a later loco with the same basic body, it is possible to use plastic card and paper to make the earlier Class 26. It is possible to buy a conversion kit, but the method shown produces the model at no more than the cost of the materials. The work is shown in the illustrations.

(1)   Carve off the small rectangular plates under the side grilles. Leave the plastic smooth, using fine emery paper if necessary.

(2)   Modify the small grilles on the right-hand side by gouging out the centre of the leading pair and shaving off the front half of the after pair.

(3)   Carve off the corresponding grilles on the opposite side.

(4)   Clean off the moulding pimple (if present) in the centre of the roof.

(5)   With thin paper held around the body, use a pencil to scribble over all the existing roof edge grilles so embossing them on to the paper — just as schoolchildren emboss pennies through paper.

(6)   This now enables you to overcome the main difference between the Class 33 and Class 26/27 bodies, the different grille dispositions. Cut out three of the embossed grilles and cement them on to the right-hand side aft behind the existing moulded grilles. Add one other embossed grille in the one gap remaining on the left-hand side run of grilles.

(7)   Now carefully scrape away the moulded grille from the front on each side, and rub down to give a smooth gap.

(8)   On the front end of the roof cut down and smooth off the existing vents in the moulded panel-hatch. Cut a new bigger hatch 24mm long by 25mm wide and glue it over the original hatch. Scrape away the paint first and then use liquid cement flooded through the paper to afix the new panel.

(9)   Now add new vents, apertures, and exhausts on the roof — see picture. Add small patches also on top of the air horn covers.

(10)   Cut out new front door panels from 10thou plastic card (see drawing). Cut away moulded trim from centres of ends, then cement the door panels in place on each nose. A thin strip of plastic card across the top edge neatly finishes off the new, reduced area, centre window surround.

(11)   Remove marker lights carefully — the dummy lenses are a force fit, cut out new card discs and drill new positions for the marker light lenses under the screen windows.

(12)   Punch out four discs from paper and glue them in place as marker discs on each nose, folding in half horizontally those which are not to be displayed. Note that the centre pair were originally offset to the left (viewed head-on) when the nose doors opened. As the doors are welded up at refit the centre discs are usually moved to the centre line — check the loco you are modelling.

Right:
The completed model numbered as No 26034 after repainting.

(13)   Punch out more discs this time from card and cement over the original buffer heads which are far too small.

(14)   Use 20thou plastic card to blank off the door windows.

(15)   Add a new water tank on to the belly by cementing a 22mm by 10mm rectangle over the Class 33 tank. Add a 22mm by 5mm overlay, and a small disc to depict a filler cap.

(16)   Add screen wipers (from Bambi staples) trimmed and bent to shape.

(17)   Use guitar G string snippets for the heat and vacuum brake pipes in suitably drilled holes on the buffer beam each side of the moulded coupler hook.

(18)   Add 'mini' snowploughs if desired. They are optional, but they frequently are carried all year round by most locomotives. If you retain the tension-lock couplers make simplified ploughs, and cement them behind the coupler. If you use any other type of smaller coupler the ploughs will need to be made rather bigger, as in the prototype illustrations of the Class 26.

(19)   Most Class 26 locos had a plate added over the air horn grille, to keep out rain and snow. A strip of plastic card simulates this on the model.

(20)   Lastly, snip through the top of the vertical side pillar on the cab side window, bend it back to match the front screen rake, and cement it firmly. These locos have a sliding pane of glass here, not a drop pane as on the Class 33.

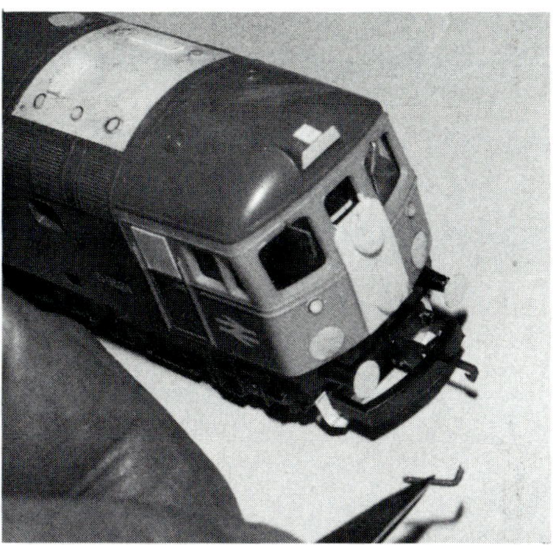

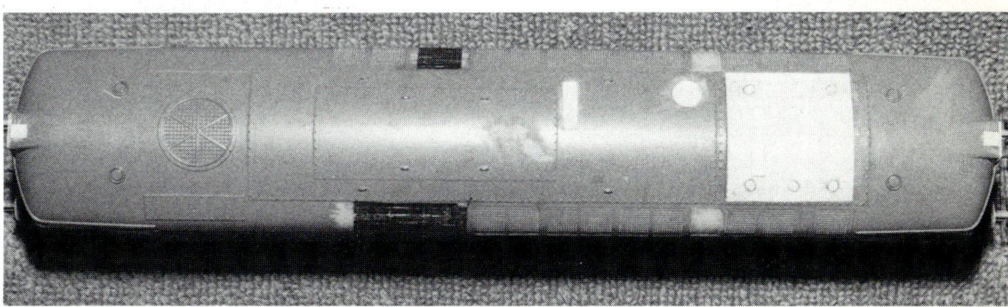

Above:
Stages in converting the Class 33 to a Class 26, all as described in the text.

Class 110 DMU (Hornby model)

This is the three-car DMU set by Hornby which is done in the attractive 'refurbished' livery. It is a very fine model as it comes, but it lends itself to some extra detailing and it can be converted to EM gauge. The method shown here for EM conversion can be applied to all Hornby diesel locos.

Right:
Converting the set to EM is extremely easy, but start with the trailer car and the non-powered driving car. The bogies are easily removed by prising out the lugs which hold them in place — use a small screwdriver as a lever. The Hornby wheels are then simply removed and EMGS/ Ultrascale coach disc wheel sets are directly substituted. The bogies are then replaced. Here we see the non-powered car after conversion and running on Scaleway Code 75 EM track. The brake shoes on the bogies now line up exactly on the wheel rims and need a slight filling to ensure they do not actually touch the rims.

Left:
Now turn to the power car and dis-assemble this by releasing the lugs which separate the body from the chassis. The instruction sheet with the set shows where the lugs are positioned. Release the two bogies, unclip the leads, and separate the bogie frames from the metal centres. On the pick-up bogie open out the wheels to EM back-to-back by holding each pair in a small vice and tapping in the axle by about 1mm on each side. Use the EMGS back-to-back gauge to check the correct wheel setting, then put a pin size blob of glue into each axle hole to hold the wheel firmly on to the axle. Now re-assemble the bogie and test it for running on EM track and turn-outs.

Right:
On the powered bogie take the side frames and carefully carve away 2mm of depth from the inside of the axle boxes on the side with the plain wheels (ie, without the traction tyres). Make it neat. Though the cuts do not show outside the bogie, any rough work may obstruct wheel clearance. Remove the wheels on the power bogie by pulling off those on the non-insulated side. Put the remaining wheel and axle in the vice and tap in the axle by about 1mm. Then re-assemble the axles to the motor block and push on the removed wheels, adjusting the back-to-back for EM by using the EM gauge. Use Evo-stik in the axle holes to ensure the gauge stays fixed. The geared wheels remain in their original (OO gauge) positions relative to the drive from the motor, but the wider wheel track throws the bogie itself slightly off-centre.

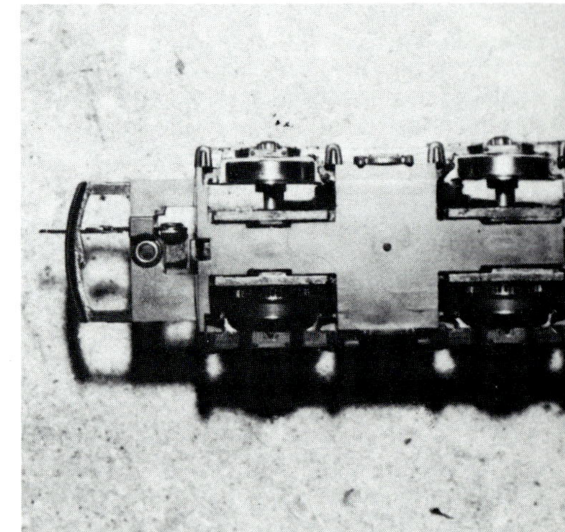

Right:
Having re-gauged for EM you have a 'lop-sided' bogie, but it is not noticeable when the train is on the track. However, the most important point is to ensure the drive wheels stay in position to engage the motor drive and this is done by cementing 2mm wide strips of plastic card or scrap plastic inside the bogie frames to stop the geared wheels moving too far sideways.

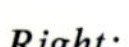

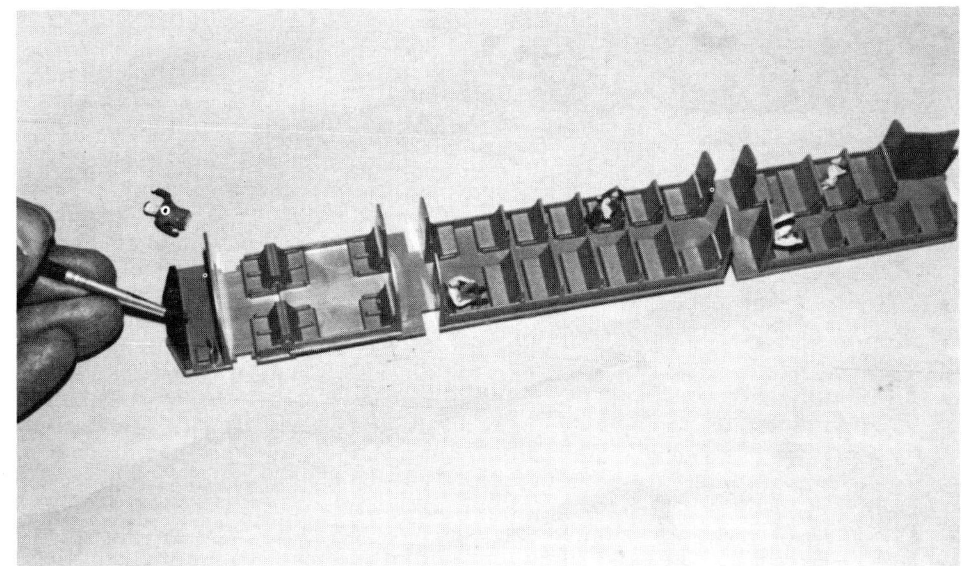

Take each car body apart in turn, remove the interior, paint inside as you desire, eg bulkheads and driving cab interior as here. Add some suitable figures to sit on some of the seats. This can be done with all models of passenger stock.

Below:
Now add the few missing details. Here we see a speedometer box (just below the WY emblem) and the cable to the front axle made from Microrod. It is NOT attached to the bogie. Use plastic card strip to make guard irons and 8mm × 2mm steps. Two are needed below each driver's and guard's door, glued in place on the bogie sides. Another view of the front end, showing plastic card steps and the MU and brake and heat piping on the front. Note also the dummy coupler and the lamp irons added on the buffers. Cut away the front coupler mount from the bogie.

Left:
The final detail added was a tiny air horn just below and alongside the right buffer mounting at each front end. Plastic scrap can be filed to shape. All new additions were then painted to match the appropriate colours of the underframe. Very light application of wear and weathering was made. 'First', 'No Smoking' and overhead warning signs were added from SMS transfers sheet A11 (but Kemco also do the right sort). This close view shows part of the completed set with EM wheels, passengers and signs, and light weathering.

Above:
An excellent example of a conversion job. Chris Leigh produces the cast metal and etched parts enabling the Class 117 power car by Lima to be easily converted to either the Class 121 or Class 122 single unit railcars.
S. W. Stevens-Stratten

Above:
The Lima Class 117 DMU with modifications and added detail. The model as purchased and straight out-of-the-box is in the background, while the one as detailed by Chris Leigh is in the foreground. Note the front end treatment and the fact that the modified one sits lower on its bogies. *S. W. Stevens-Stratten*

5 Rolling stock

Passenger rolling stock is no problem for the modeller of modern British Rail. The proprietary manufacturers have between them covered nearly all the BR standard types in common use.

The famous Mk 1 coaches of 1951-62 are still in service at the time of writing, but most are due for withdrawal and in 1984 the majority of those running were only used on secondary services. Lima, Hornby and Mainline make 4mm scale examples of all types, but it is worth pointing out that the Mainline buffet-restaurant coach is the only catering stock model with an accurate roof and underframe, for the other manufacturers make do with their standard coach roofs and chassis. Because recent prototype construction has concentrated on coach types a fair number of Mk 1 sleeping cars, restaurant cars and full brakes were still to be seen on main line services even in the 1980s.

In N scale there are excellent Mk 1 coaches from Hornby-Minitrix and from Graham Farish, the latter being particularly good as they have an accurate flush window finish.

There are differences to be observed in models of Mk 1 passenger stock. As originally produced a bogie of 'traditional' type was fitted, designated BR1. This proved to have somewhat rough-riding qualities especially after some wear had taken place. To improve the ride two different designs were evolved by about 1960. One was the BR4 bogie, distinguished by its girder-style side frames and prominent springs, and the other design was the Commonwealth bogie, a cast frame type of American appearance. Many coaches were fitted with these improved bogies on refurbishment. Whilst the BR1 bogie is still to be seen, well into the 1980s, most Mk 1 coaches retained in service have the BR4 or Commonwealth bogies. Models are produced with all three types of bogie and, obviously, the BR4 and Commonwealth bogie models are to be preferred for a layout set in recent years. In most cases bogies can be changed around to give the desired combination.

For many years Mk 1 catering coaches were found in trains otherwise composed of

Below:
An excellent model of modern rolling stock is this VIX van from Hornby in 4mm scale.

Mk 2 stock since the latter coaches were restricted to standard passenger vehicles. The Mk 2 stock built in the 1963-73 period, was derived from the XP64 designs and features integral body and chassis rather than a separate chassis as in the Mk 1. Many versions were made — Mk 2a to Mk 2c lack air conditioning and have opening windows while Mk 2d-Mk 2f are air conditioned and thus have sealed window frames. Hornby make a Mk 2 coach, Lima a Mk 2a and Airfix (now taken over by Mainline) make Mk 2d-Mk 2e air conditioned coaches for 4mm scale. Until a Mk 3 type came along in the early 1980s, InterCity sleepers were of the Mk 1 type. Lima have now produced a Mk 3 sleeper which they have released in 4mm scale in 1984.

The latest type of coach for principal loco-hauled trains and the HST is the Mk 3 and this is a slick new 75ft long design. They have comfortable air-conditioned interiors and are cleared for fast running up to 125mph. The body shell is common for all types but the interior varies with different uses — ie between first- and second-class etc. Lima and Hornby both make Mk 3 coaches in 4mm scale, but the latter models are one bay short although they still manage to look convincing. Jouef of France also made a Mk 3 (both first- and second-class) coach which were excellent, but unfortunately they are no longer manufactured and are now difficult to obtain. In N scale Graham Farish make a full range of Mk 3 coaches. All the Mk 3 models which are sold separately come with buffers which are added for loco-hauled trains but should be omitted if the coach forms part of a HST set.

In the coaching stock category come luggage vans. In 4mm scale Lima produce a GUV (general utility van), a CCT (covered carriage truck) and a full brake Mk 1. Of these the first two are excellent but the full brake is actually too long for scale since it utilises the standard passenger coach roof

Above:

**An illustration of the prototype VEA van —
compare the chassis with the model photograph .**
Paul W. Bartlett

Left:

**A VEA 12-ton corrugated end box van, an
example of an older 10ft wheelbase van in modern
Railfreight livery by Hornby. The body is
accurate but the chassis is entirely wrong.**

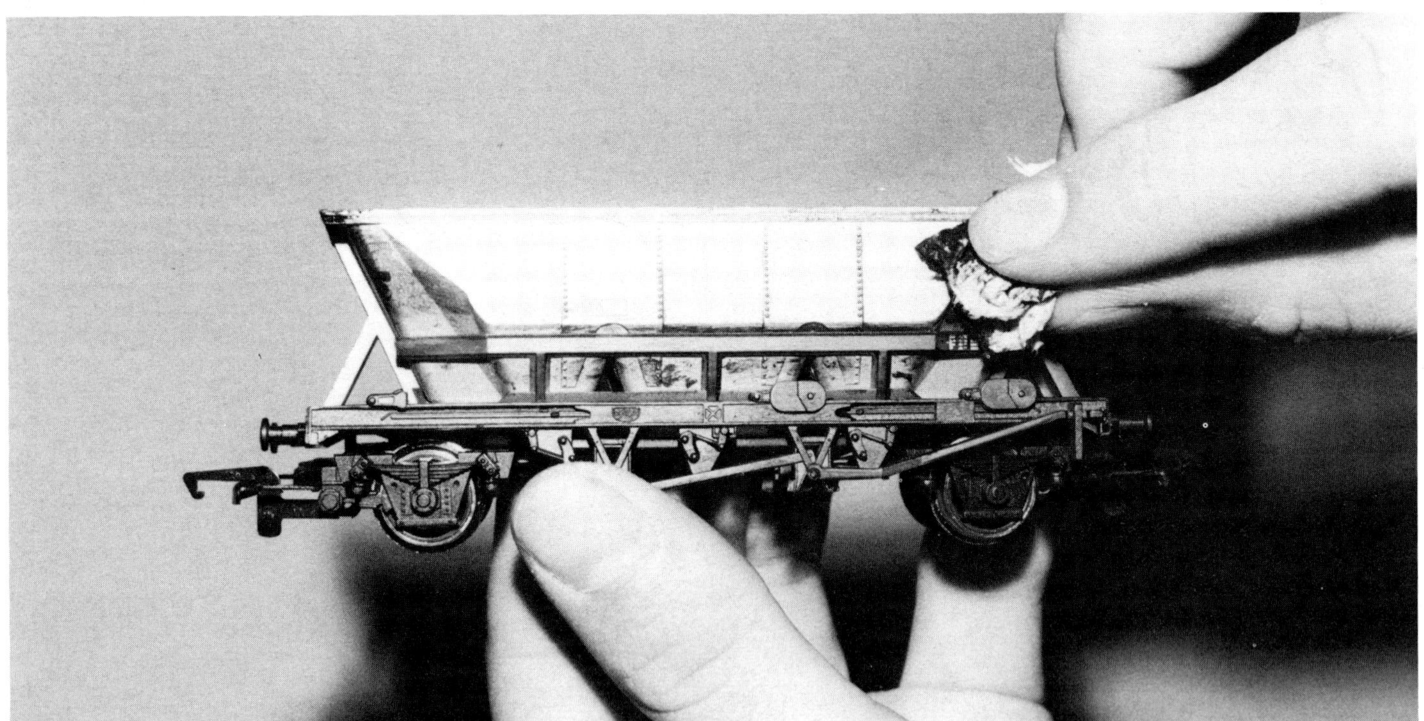

Top:
Improving a Hornby model; this SAA steel wagon is transformed in appearance when its heavy Hornby wheels are replaced by scale blackened wheelsets and all the bright fixings of the tension-lock coupler are painted over matt black.

Centre:
Hornby HAA and Lima Procor stone hopper are typical modern wagons available ready-to-run. When suitably dirtied as shown above and fitted with scale wheels they are superbly realistic. Even the tension lock couplings look less conspicuous after being toned down with dirt colour paint.

Above:
Hornby HAA merry-go-round hopper needs dirtying for a typical in-service appearance. A quick way of doing this is to paint, one side at a time, matt black and then quickly wipe off the paint with a tissue. Repeat as necessary and vary with dark earth colour. Note scale wheels are fitted, a simple substitution using Wheelwrights, Alan Gibson, or any of the other makes of scale wheelsets available.

and underframe. Lima produce the ex-GWR Syphon G which was seen until 1981-2 in many parcels and newspaper trains. They also make the ex-LMSR full brake, and Mainline make the 50ft full brake (ex-LMSR which was still to be seen in the 1980s). Various old pre-nationalisation coaches and passenger vans are still in departmental use and a few items, like the old boarded-side SR GUVs are to be seen in limited service apart from use in engineering trains. Since BR eliminated their traditional 'door-to-door' parcels service in 1982 there has been wholesale scrapping of redundant vehicles and lines of them marked 'condemned' were a familiar sight in 1982-3 indicating a possible scenic use for an old model van on a modern layout.

Freight Stock

For many years British Railways freight trains presented a drab appearance of browns and greys, all liberally covered in dirt and the typical wagon was a small hand-braked four-wheeler clanking along with loose couplings in a slow moving train. Some of these old wagons may still be seen around, but there has been a major transformation in the last 10 years or so, and exciting new wagons have appeared which have broken away from what was, in effect, 19th century technology and given BR some stock which matches the quality of modern freight vehicles in Europe or the USA.

The new generation of vehicles gives higher capacity and higher speeds. The aim, nearly achieved, is to have all trains braked throughout and there has been much rationalisation of freight operation to streamline the system.

All new wagon designs are air-braked and the old vacuum brake is on its way out. A fully fitted (ie braked throughout) train has no brake van but a train with both air and vacuum braked wagons will have one — for while the air braked wagons are arranged next to the locomotive the vacuumed braked wagons at the end are effectively unbraked so the brake van is required. Brake vans will otherwise be found only on permanent way trains or 'specials' such as those carrying toxic chemicals. In the absence of the brake van, by the way, the guard rides in the rear cab of the diesel or electric locomotive.

For a long time the supply of modern freight vehicles was poor in the ready-to-run field, but in recent years there have been great strides in 4mm scale from Hornby and Lima. These two firms have produced a remarkably good selection of 'new genera-tion' stock and provide nearly all that is necessary to reproduce modern operations in miniature. Hornby offer the VEA ventilated van, VDA 45-ton van, OBA 45-ton wagon, VIX ferry wagon and SAA steel wagon, plus the HAA merry-go-round hopper. They also make Freightliner container flats, car trans-porter flats, a 100-ton tank wagon and a modern style tank wagon in several liveries. These are all key types. Lima add to this with a Procor stone hopper in several private owner liveries and a Procor 82-tonne pallet van (PWA), also, in several private owner liveries as well as BR livery. They also offer a 100-tonne Class A tanker in several liveries, a Procor 45-ton grain hopper wagon and a bogie ore wagon.

In the Mainline/Airfix ranges there are a few older types which are applicable to the modern scene, including a Lowmac machinery wagon, a 21-ton hopper, and the 16-ton mineral wagon which Mainline model on an incorrect 10ft wheelbase chassis. Quite unintentionally they created a model depict-ing one of the later rebuilds by BR which put 16-ton mineral wagon bodies on to 10ft

Below:
The same dirtying treatment being applied to a Lima CCT. The roof has already been treated and dark earth paint has been applied to the side and is now being wiped off while still wet. Scale wheels have been substituted.

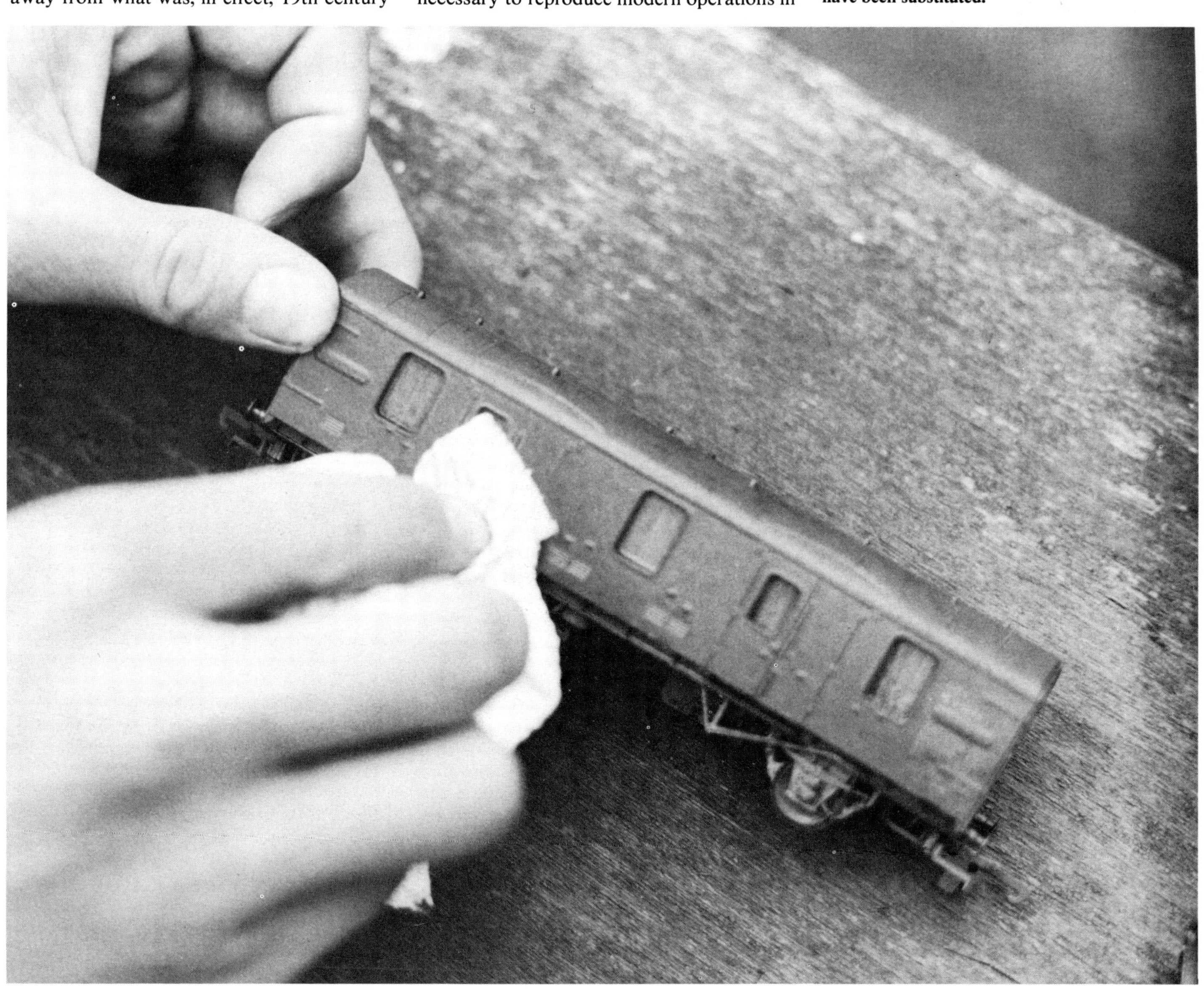

wheelbase chassis to give an acceptable type for modern operations. A tie-bar joining the axle boxes is the main requirement. Brake vans in modern finish are also included in the Mainline/Airfix range.

From all this it will be seen that the 4mm scale modeller is extremely lucky and well served. Bearing in mind that block trains are most often run today the biggest restraint on the modeller is likely to be financial — the money needed to buy 30 HAAs for a scale length merry-go-round coal train for instance!

The N scale enthusiast is much less well served at the time of writing — although signs are that things are improving. Hornby-Minitrix offer a HAA coal hopper but have a 16-ton mineral wagon, a box van and BR brake van which just about scrape in as old types still to be seen. Lima offer a Freight-liner container flat and Peco have a good number of tankers, pallet vans, and others in modern private owner or Speedlink livery — though these represent the 1960s vintage as they appear today, rather than the later designs. None of this comes near to matching the wealth of types for 4mm but N gauge versions of the principal types like the VIX and VDA must surely come. Graham Farish produce Freightliner container flats and 100-ton tank wagons, with other modern types scheduled.

The 7mm scale modeller has nothing at all in either kit or ready-to-run form at the time

of writing as far as modern wagons are concerned, so it would be a matter of scratch-building. However, the appearance of good modern O gauge loco and coach kits from David Parkin in recent times suggests that someone soon *must* market some modern BR wagon kits as well.

Departmental Stock

The 4mm scale modeller is again well served by Lima and Hornby. Hornby offer a crane and track cleaner vehicle in the guise of an engineering coach, while Lima have an

Top:
Colourful Private Owner tanker liveries added to the Peco N gauge range in 1983 are, again, typical of 1980s stock though these depict 1960s designs still in service rather than the latest type of tank wagon.

Above:
Watch for jokers — though this Freightliner container flat looks rather good made up in a train it is actually bogus and does not depict an actual prototype. There are a few models around like this which are good enough products but not strictly scale replicas. This one is from Hornby.

Top:
Very good Mk 1 coaches are produced for N gauge by Graham Farish. Wheel rims when painted black will improve the looks still further.

Above:
Though rather spartan and in need of detailing on the underframe, this Hornby Freightliner container flat is a more acceptable 4mm scale model.

Below:
A correctly made up InterCity 125 HST using Lima and Jouef stock (the latter only for trailer seconds pending release of the Lima versions), all correctly detailed on the layout of Richard Elwen. The choice of the NE-SW train formation makes the best use of available stock. *Richard Elwen*

engineering department coach, air compressor van and various Enparts and tools, all correctly done as former fleet vehicles and appropriately repainted and marked. Lima have also produced 4mm scale models of the Sealion and Seacow ballast wagons.

The N scale modellers, apart from a Lima Enparts van, have very little on the market at the present time and they will have to repaint and/or adapt existing older items.

Transfers

Various firms including Kemco manufacture marking sheets appropriate to British Rail in their range of transfers and these make the provision of data panels, or altering of codes or numbers an easy matter.

Right:
Airfix/Mainline Mk 2d coaches are superb models for 4mm scale and run freely. This one has been lightly weathered and the tension-lock coupling has been replaced by an American Kadee magnetic knuckle coupler, duplicating the coupling arrangement on the real coaches. Tension-lock couplers may be left on the outer ends of the sets of coaches to couple to locos, but the knuckle couplers give a realistic close coupling.

Below:
Here is a good way to add a modernised mineral wagon to a modern BR stock collection. BR rebuilt many old 16-ton mineral wagons by moving the bodies on to 10ft wheelbase piped underframes left over from scrapped pallet vans and other redundant vehicles. This gave the mineral wagons a new lease of life with their old 9ft wheelbase underframes now replaced. Mainline make their 16tonner on the standard 10ft wheelbase chassis, a production simplification which can be turned to advantage. Add a tie-bar and door-stops from plastic card, and thicken the top centre beading, and you have a modernised 16tonner (TOPS code MCU) suitable for any present day setting.

6 Operations

The rail traveller of the steam age might find little superficial difference in today's British Rail passenger operations. There are new and modernised stations, but many stations are substantially the same as they were in the days of steam. There are new forms of traction — electric and diesel — and the colours and styles are different. But there is still the bustle at the stations, the announcements, the mail loadings, the taxi ranks outside the station, piles of luggage, and a general flurry of activity as trains come and go. Even the traditional station pilot locomotive will be seen handling empty coaching stock at principal stations. Missing from the scene of yesteryear are milk churns, pigeon specials, livestock in general, and parcels, all of these forms of traffic having been abandoned by BR at various times over the years. There are generally fewer posters, brighter lights, more car park space, and cleaner buildings (even old 'smokey' buildings have been cleaned to show up at their best). But in the larger stations there may still be a branch or suburban train in the bay, principal expresses at the main platforms, and trains of vans, just as there always have been. In creating a model scene, therefore, it is largely a matter of getting the details right, with believable train formations, and anyone who started off modelling the steam scene won't be at a loss for actually running the trains. Indeed it would be a very interesting project to update an existing 'steam age' layout to the present day by changing all the signs and posters, eliminating unwanted tracks or facilities (eg, coaling stage, water crane), just as BR actually did.

In real life, needless to say, the changes have been rather more fundamental, and that is quite apart from the changes in modes of traction. Over the years timetables have been considerably revised for passenger services, partly due to the elimination of some services, but mostly due to the greatly increased speed which electric and diesel haulage has made possible. The celebrated, and now familiar, High Speed Train has revolutionised principal services on the non-electrified main line routes of the Western, Midland, and Eastern Regions.

Similarly electric traction has increased speeds and services on those lines which have been electrified, notably those on the old Great Eastern system and the London Midland Region which were actually initiated in the original modernisation plan of the 1950s.

A new version of an old concept, the push-pull train, is a feature of modern British Railways that leads itself well to modelling, not least because the trains can be shorter than most passenger workings on main lines. On the Southern Region the push-pull idea was revised using the Class 33/1 (a specially adapted loco) with special 4TC four-car coach sets having control cabs at the outer

Above:
Modern DMU operation gives an excuse for a colourful mix of styles illustrated by the Graham Farish N scale Metro-Cammell sets in both the old the and blue style and the post-1978 blue/grey, both running in the same formation, which is a common sight at the time of writing.

Left:
Ideal prototype for the modern BR modeller is the West Highland line — all single track — and specifically the Kyle of Lochalsh the western end of the route. Here at the terminus in 1980 is a train composed of three Mk 1 coaches strengthened on this occasion by an extra composite, a Southern Region 'vintage' GUV, and two CCTs, headed by a Class 26 locomotive. Old 'traditional' BR freight vehicles are on the quayside line in the background. Note that the loco, still with the old headcode discs dating from 'steam age' practice is showing the single upper disc to denote a stopping passenger train, just as a steam loco should have done with its oil headcode lights 20 or so years ago.

ends. These units are used west of Bournemouth on the non-electrified section of the Waterloo-Weymouth line but are seen working through to Waterloo. The Edinburgh-Glasgow service of the Scottish Region is similarly operated as a push-pull train with a Class 47/7 and five-coach Mk 3 sets, again with a driving control cab in a specially converted Brake 2nd coach at the outer end of the set. Prior to 1980 the service was worked in effect as pull-pull with a Class 27/1 loco at each end of a Mk 2 coach set. For modelling purposes the Class 47/7 and the Mk 3 control cab coach are straightforward conversions from ready-to-run models and have been dealt with in the modelling press. The Southern Region 4TC sets are made as MTK kits and the Class 33 loco can be converted to the 33/1 variant quite easily, conversion kits being available from several makers.

Local services are provided on BR by the diesel multiple-units (DMU) and electric multiple-units (EMU). As already mentioned, in model form these are not over-generously covered and the selection is limited, however, for the average layout there is enough to suit most needs. In 4mm scale there is a Lima Class 117 DMU set, though it needs one car converting to a Motor 2nd for complete accuracy. The Class 117 Motor Brake 2nd can also be converted easily to a Class 121 or 122 single-unit railcar and a conversion kit is available from Chris Leigh which makes this work remarkably easy. Hornby have made a Class 110 DMU, and in N gauge there is a fine Metro-Cammell Class 101 from Graham Farish. There are no ready-to-run EMU sets at the time of writing, nor are there any Southern Region EMUs or DMUs — all gaps waiting to be filled. However, there are some MTK kits which can be constructed (although these are not recommended for the novice) and it is possible to convert Mk 1 coaches and add a power bogie to produce a Southern Region 4BEP (Class 410) or 4CEP (Class 411) unit, but this is not easy as the sides, window apertures and doors need quite extensive modification.

Even with the limitations noted in available models and kits, however, there is today more than enough available in terms of locomotives and stock, certainly for OO and N gauges, for all traffic requirements to be catered for, with the exception of Southern Region EMUs.

There are no real problems in running modern style passenger services and space is likely to be the greatest limitation. For example in 4mm scale a full length HST takes 7-9ft, demanding a fair sized layout if the true main line atmosphere is to be captured. This is where N gauge comes into its own, for the very good models now avail-

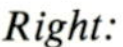

Right:
A company train modelled by Don Jones on his OO gauge garden layout. A Jouef model of a Class 40 ('Whistler') hauls a train of British Leyland cars from Longbridge to Liverpool for export shipment. *Brian Monaghan*

able in this smaller size makes this scale worthy of serious consideration for anyone wishing to depict modern main line practice — a full length N gauge HST is much less demanding of space, as is a full length 30-hopper 'merry-go-round' coal train.

For those without much space it is certainly worth dispelling the myth that modern trains are long, for there are still plenty of branch and secondary lines where short trains are very much the order of the day. There are branches using single unit railcars, while choosing a setting like the West Highland Line or lines west of Salisbury not only make short (three-five coach) trains perfectly believable but allow single track main lines to be depicted. Some freight trains are equally short and the suggested shelf layout plan included in this book, Coombe Junction, has been selected specially for those who lack space for large layouts and long trains. Freight trains with as few as six hopper wagons can be seen on this sort of branch.

Freight operation is much more varied and exciting, and certainly since the BR modernisation it has become completely different from the old traditional ways where nearly every station had a goods yard, with cattle dock and/or coal merchant's staithe as appropriate. Many modellers do not appreciate this fact, it seems, for layouts are still to be seen purporting to depict the modern era where all freight movement seems to have been in the old time style of the steam and early diesel era, and all freight trains are consequently of the pick-up or mixed goods variety.

Modern freight trains are most often characterised by the use of high capacity fully braked wagons and there are develop-

ments which positively help modellers. First, there is the 'merry-go-round' train (MGR) which serves the coal and power supply industries. Here a train of up to 30 hopper wagons (usually of the HAA type) picks up coal from tipplers at a coal mine and takes it direct to the power station or dock. The train does not stop in this operation, but it runs very, very slowly, discharging into special unloading facilities via the doors in the bottom of the hopper wagons. The train literally routes itself in a circle between two destinations. To achieve the slow speeds necessary, the locomotives used on these trains are fitted with special slow speed control equipment.

Container trains are another major aspect of BR freight operation. BR call them Freightliners and these trains handle the container traffic which now dominates world commerce. The trains run from container terminals situated near major towns and at (or near) the major seaports. All the terminals have good road connections for the local collection and distribution of the containers and a feature of these is the giant cranes which straddle the railway tracks for lifting and placing the containers on the flat railway wagons. Another feature is the stacks of 20ft and 40ft long standard containers which are owned by Freightliners (a BR subsidiary) or by private owners, who usually have their names well displayed. In miniature container traffic can be a most attractive feature, well catered for by Hornby and Lima in 4mm scale. Lima make an inexpensive container terminal which is hand operated, while Faller make a more expensive powered container gantry crane and Noch make a container lifting adapter to fit Marklin and other powered cranes, but the latter two items are in HO scale. In N scale Lima can also offer both the containers and a small terminal.

Another major modern category is the company train. These are block trains for such materials as aggregate, ore, limestone, oil, consumer goods, cars and car components etc. In fact, around 65% of BR's freight traffic (excluding coal) is conveyed in privately owned wagons and there are private sidings to cater for this sort of traffic and these are on the increase. In most cases the wagons for private use are leased from firms like Procor or BRT (a BR leasing organisation) and the modern hoppers made for Procor used by firms like Amey Roadstone are well known — Lima make the 4mm scale model. Private sidings to operate these trains are often very simple, sometimes just literally a double-ended siding, and this really helps the modeller. Included in the 'private' category are coal concentration depots, owned by firms like Charrington or Coalite, where coal in bulk is shipped in by rail for distribution by road. Small oil fuel depots (sometimes only for central heating oil) also exist, another small operation which is ideal for modelling.

Trunk route freight trains operate under the Speedlink name. These trains are timetable operations linking main industrial areas and offering, usually, overnight service running at up to 75mph. They are composed of sets of vans and wagons, fully air-braked and running from freight terminals where customers may deliver by road, or from

Above left:
Here is a merry-go-round train, hauled by a Class 47 loco, moving very slowly through the loading shed at Kellingley Colliery. For modellers this is quite an easy proposition for the structure is merely a concrete block building with a corrugated 'shed' at the top.
National Coal Board

Left:
The building for the unloading is even easier for the modeller as it is a simple structure with windows on the first floor which houses the control gear. This is at Immingham, South Humberside with a train unloading via below surface 'pits' from which the coal is carried by conveyor belt to the stacking area seen on the right of the illustration. *BR/Ian Allan Library*

Above:
The first of the Class 56 locos passing through Worksop with a heavy m-g-r train in May 1981. Note the old style station building now bearing modern style signs and lamps and the Victorian type footbridge. *John Wright*

Right:
The classic Freightliner terminal, this one at Southampton Maritime with a train of container flats being loaded. The operation can be duplicated in miniature with the Lima or Faller cranes. *BR/Ian Allan Library*

Freightliner
Load 26640 KGS
58740 LBS
Tare 3840 KGS
8460 LBS
Capacity 67cum
2366cuft
GO BUY MERCEDES-BENZ TRUCKS
MBH 799V
SCANIA
B1
TTM 125W

private sidings where traffic is regular. Speedlink trains also run from marshalling yards and connect with the train ferries at Dover and Harwich with export/import traffic.

There are still local trains on trip working, particularly in industrial areas, which bring in wagons from outlying districts to freight terminals or marshalling yards, but the old type of non-fitted freight train and pick-up goods has virtually disappeared. The new Railfreight livery of flame red and grey is fast coming in, though there are still many vehicles in the older liveries to be seen.

Engineering trains are commonly seen reballasting or relaying track or attending at the scene of civil engineering works. Plasser equipment used in such engineering work is not available in ready-to-run form (except by Liliput in HO scale), but articles on how to make it have appeared in the model railway press and in the *Model Railway Constructor Annual* for 1983. For 4mm scale, Lima are producing the Sealion and Seacow ballast hoppers, and as various old wagons are pressed into departmental use for carrying rail sleepers and ballast, it is not difficult to depict a modern Permanent Way train.

Until recently (1981), BR also ran a door-to-door parcels service. This usually utilised the old goods sheds at main BR stations, although occasionally bay platforms were used within passenger stations. Covered vans of all types — full brakes, CCT, GUVs, etc — were utilised. BR closed down this service however, as an economy measure and this resulted in the mass scrapping of vans and the virtual disappearance of parcels traffic trains with the exception of certain contract workings.

Top left:
Lack of space for a container handling crane gantry need not prevent Freightliner operations on a small layout. This simple siding terminal uses a Kranmobil box handler to lift containers from the rail flat wagons to the road vehicles alongside, and vice-versa. Lima produce a different container crane which can be used in a similar way — all you need is a siding and the handling crane. Lorries in 4mm scale are available in kit form manufactured by Scankits and available at many model shops. *John Reed*

Left:
Freightliner trains can be very short. Though eight flats are being hauled here through Goring by No 47109, as few as three would not be incorrect. *John Chalcraft*

Top:
An Engineer's ballast train, again very short, and with a LMSR type brake van, is here laying ballast on a quiet Sunday in May 1976. This sort of working is very much the province of lower powered locos like the Class 31 shown here, the Class 25, and for the Southern Region the Class 73. *BR/Ian Allan Library*

Above:
HST power cars can sometimes be seen running as 'light engine' just like any other diesel loco, offering a good excuse to run HST power cars on 'test runs', even on a small layout. However, this failed unit is being shunted by No 08483 air-braked, buck-eye coupled HST shunter at Marsh Junction Bristol in July 1980. Note the panel carrying the number has been lifted and a tow—bar attached. *C. G. Maggs*

7 Along the Lineside

Probably the easiest of all aspects of modelling for the modern BR era is the matter of linesides and structures. Essentially the changes depend on local conditions. The changes in traffic patterns and motive power clearly saw the wholesale demolition and selling of unwanted freight yards, engine sheds, goods sheds, and so on. This sometimes means that freight sheds are seen in isolation converted for business use but no longer connected with tracks. Around most stations the old goods yard is concreted over and used as a car park with the appropriate notices. At the biggest stations there will be a hut for an attendant but more often than not there is a tariff notice with the admonition to pay at the booking office, or at a 'pay-and-display' type meter. In some cases the land has been sold for development.

The old style of loco shed is replaced by modern diesel sheds (Hornby make a good one), with refuelling points, but often these days diesel locos are left in the open at stabling points. This may be nothing more than a siding left over from the old goods yards when the other sidings were lifted, or it may be a disused bay platform road in the station. Therefore, on a small layout a loco department of the traditional sort could be omitted — so saving valuable space.

Many signalboxes have been eliminated and demolished following the coming of centralised control, and some of the new signalboxes don't look like the traditional boxes — rather, they resemble any other light industrial building or office. The old style of gated level crossing has also gone and barriers replace it. A detail to remember, however, is an adjacent concrete post carrying a remote TV camera to watch the crossing if it is not near a box. Occasionally ungated crossings with the international 'cross-buck' sign and a prominent warning board may be encountered on little-used lines.

Station buildings may have been swept away and replaced by new industrial style building structures, or they may be demolished on one platform only or replaced by a 'bus shelter' type installation for waiting passengers. However, recently it has been more common to refurbish or restore the original structure (some of which may have a preservation order anyway), and sometimes modern structures or additions are blended in. Some of these offer distinct improvements on the originals in fact.

On branch lines, platforms may actually be truncated or new modern sectionalised concrete platforms may be built (the basic Airfix station platform is actually a good likeness for this). There are many cases of new stations that need to meet changing traffic patterns — for example Bristol Parkway which provides a stop at the important city of Bristol without diverting the principal South Wales trains into Bristol itself. Some of the Passenger Transport Executives set up by the Metropolitan Counties have also been active in building new stations to serve new housing estates or business areas and most of these authorities now have their own symbol on the trains which run under their auspices.

Many new small huts have appeared in recent years, blending in with traditional old platelayer's huts and there is no firm rule for this. The Portakabin is very much part of the modern scene (as are stacks of pallets at freight terminals, together with fork-lift trucks and other handling equipment).

Signalling is an aspect of model railways which usually comes low down in the list of priorities, at least as far as many layouts are concerned. It is true that there are layouts to be seen which have full working signalling systems installed, protecting crossings and turn-outs in prototype fashion. And several manufacturers, including Fleischmann and Jouef, produce ready-to-install signal systems as part of the block systems freely available within their ranges and fully described in their catalogues. They produce all the necessary isolating tracks, switches and wiring, plus the colour light signals, though naturally these are of European prototype and any modeller of the modern British scene would need to make some cosmetic changes to make the signals more closely resemble British types. The fact remains, however, that relatively few modellers bother to install properly detailed and wired signal systems and physical limitations have much to do with it, for if you have only a small layout of the terminus-to-fiddle yard variety there may only be room for one or two signals in the length between the station platform and the visual end of the

A pleasing modern operation is a 'Park and Ride' scheme which keeps road traffic out of St Ives (Cornwall). Visitors park at Lelant Saltings for a fee which includes train travel for all the car occupants to St Ives. A purpose built platform has been built but with no shelter. The train, a DMU, shuttles between St Erth, Lelant Saltings, Carbis Bay and St Ives. *D. Percival*

Right:

The new station at St Ives is but a shadow of the original building and now consists of a platform and a small shelter with a ticket collecting hut at the end. The original station site is given over to a car park. The shuttle service is operated by Class 117 DMU or a Class 121 railcar, and at busy periods by both. *Brian Morrison*

Right:
The old mixed with the new all over modern BR. Here is a Victorian corn merchant's warehouse once served by a private siding and looking much as it must have done in 1900, complete with faded lettering. Today it is an Engineering Department store and some of their old Conflats, used for carrying rail, are in the siding.

layout. Complication for the British modeller is that there is no system-wide standardis-ation. There are still secondary lines where the old style manual signalboxes remain, usually controlling semaphore signals dating back to the grouping era.

Gradually, however, centralised control is taking over, with the elimination of the old manual signalboxes and the semaphore signals. Multiple colour light signalling will eventually be universal. On most main Inter-City main line routes, certainly those out of London, the new centralised control system has been operating for some time. Using modern electronic technology, routes can be selected and controlled, with train move-ments monitored, over very long distances. Alternatively complex areas can be con-trolled by one signalbox, as at Euston where well over 500 route possibilities are monitored and controlled in three miles. On the most recently re-signalled route in the early 1980s, the Bedford-St Pancras route, a radio-telephone system is linked with the track circuiting so that trains can be pin-pointed very precisely by the controller.

This page and right:
Coombe Junction as it was in 1982 is an ideal subject for any modeller wanting a simple yet busy layout for a shelf type set-up in a minimal space. Traffic includes a DMU or railcar for Liskeard to Looe service and company trains serving the lime works at Moorswater. By 1983 the track plan was further simplified and was less interesting from a model point of view. The GWR signal box was demolished in favour of a ground frame. The station platform and small shelter is particularly easy to model from available kits.
Richard Gardner

Coombe Junction — two ways to reproduce it as a shelf-type layout

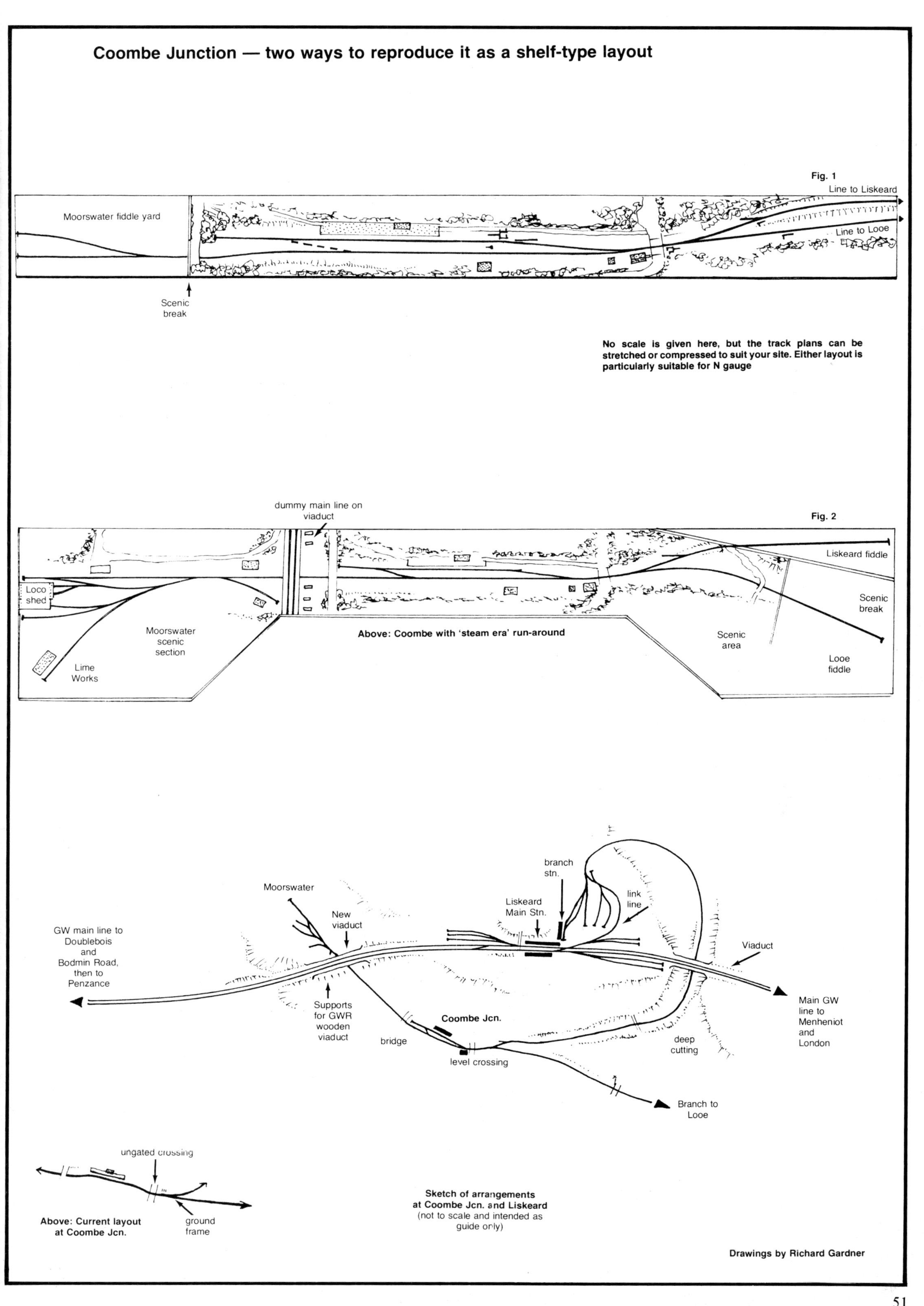

Left:
Almost all the older structures can be used in modern settings. Hornby manufacture a range for N scale and here is the engine shed, ideal for a diesel depot with a Graham Farish model of the Class 20 to show the size.

Right:
The bay platform at Woking, like many other stations, is used for the receipt and despatch of mail. Note the portable ramps to allow Post Office trolleys to be taken inside the vans. This scene, with three CCTs is ideal for duplication in miniature.

Below and below right:
Bridgend is just one of many examples of a modernised station retaining refurbished original buildings. The classic GWR offices are tastefully restored and a new modern booking hall is added together with a car park. The modern waiting room is on the opposite platform and the original GWR footbridge is retained but note the modern tall lights. *BR*

From the modellers' point of view these recent developments can be beneficial. For example, the modern systems allow single track operation without the old requirement for a token, while bi-directional running on the often simplified track layout within station areas may be permitted, the track being signalled in each direction. Old style manual signalboxes are usually demolished where the new system is installed, but they may be just boarded up and abandoned, or turned into other uses, such as tool stores — all scenic possibilities for a modern layout.

Best of all you need not feel obliged to show the physical presence of a signal cabin on your layout, for with the modern control system it might well be 50 miles away!

When it comes to installing signals there may be problems. For a route where the old manual block system is supposed to be in operation, then conventional signal models are readily available and may be used as required. Firms like Ratio offer GWR, BR, and LMS patterns, and most common signal types can be found among the small specialist manufacturers, and also available

are the usual track side and speed restriction signs which are equally applicable to modern operations. If your layout is to depict the modernised centralised control signalling, however, then authentic four-aspect colour light signals are hard to find. There are plenty of nondescript two, three, and four-aspect model signals, but relatively few that resemble actual BR patterns. Cockrobin probably has the best range, but some of their working colour light signals duplicate pre-nationalisation patterns (such as SR). It would not be impossible to build non-

working dummies of modern BR four-aspect light signals if you decide to have 'cosmetic' signals only on your layout. One scenic tip is that when a modern centralised colour light signal system is installed, the old semaphore posts may be left standing for some time after removal of their signal arms — a good way of signifying that your layout is still in the throes of modernisation!

One area not well covered is the provision of miniature station staff in the latest type of BR uniform. If such figures were available they were not easy to find at the time of writing. Some modellers have overcome this, however, by using World War 2 figures of German Afrika Korps, or at least their heads and upper torsos, since the German cap and blouse resembles the BR garment well enough in 4mm scale.

Signs in the standard BR style are included in the Tiny Signs and Lithoplans, and SMS ranges, but can also be made up from matching Letraset. Also useful are some items in the Mabex range of transfers. These include BR signs and symbols but also some useful signs like taxis, 'No parking' etc as painted on the tarmac in station yards.

Top:
It took BR some time to get around to installing the new style lettering and signs all over the system. On the West Highland line it was 1979 before the new signs appeared and here is seen the old and the new, with an incorrect spelling on the newer sign. *D. E. Brittain-Catlin*

Above:
Many old station structures have been demolished and replaced with much simpler office/entrance buildings in modern prefabricated panel style. This is Slade Green (Southern Region), again, showing the use of the standard alphabet and symbol. *BR/Ian Allan Library*

Right:
Typical of new style stations. This is Cogan on the Barry line after conversion to an unmanned halt, with bay road lifted, new lamps, old buildings removed and new ultra-simple waiting shelters substituted in local stone, easy enough to model in any scale. *BR/Ian Allan Library*

8 Suppliers

There are many small firms producing nameplates suitable for modern diesel and electric locomotives classes and among these are CGW, Kings Cross and LFC. Most large model shops stock a selection but new additions are constantly being produced and new firms appear. It is best to keep up with what is available at any given time by reference to the small advertisements in the model railway press. Sometimes new nameplates are produced very quickly — for example, CGW were offering nameplates for HST power cars in 1983 only a month after the first unit had been named.

The output of the principal model railway manufacturers is covered in the main body of this book. Models by Hornby, Lima, Mainline (Palitoy) — who also produce some of the old Airfix range — Peco and Graham Farish are available in most good toy and model shops and the firms concerned issue new catalogues frequently which illustrate and list their current products. There are smaller firms, however, whose products are not widely available in the retail trade, but who have something specific to offer those modelling modern British Rail. Much that is generally available is not specifically BR period, but is applicable in any case to BR layouts.

Adpak (28 Cottesbrook Close, Ernsford Grange, Coventry). Conversion and detailing kits for 4mm scale diesel locos.

Derek Ascott (Kirklinton, Worth, North Sussex). Cast metal scale bogie sides for Lima gauge O Class 33 loco and many useful 7mm scale components.

CGW (Crown House, 21 High Street, Billingborough, Sleaford, Lincs). 4mm nameplates.

Cockrobin Controls (106 Drove Road, Weston-super-Mare, Avon). Signals in 4mm and N gauge and control gear etc.

Craftsman Models (35 Willoughby Road, Slough, Berks). Conversion and detailing kits for 4mm scale diesel locos.

Alan Gibson (The Bungalow, Church Road, Lingwood, Norwich, Norfolk). 4mm scale wheels for diesel locos, coaches etc.

Hadley Hobbies (Middlesex Street, London EC1). Importers of JV Catenary and general model shop.

Kemco (82 Delce Road, Rochester, Kent). Range of 4mm scale transfers for BR including lining.

Kemp Models (154 Church Road, Hove, East Sussex). Distributor for Kean Maygib, Anchoridge Motors, SMS Transfers, Portescap motors, most kit manufacturers etc also general models.

King's Cross — Model Railway Manufacturing Co (14 York Way, King's Cross, London N1). Etched nameplates, kits and general models.

Langley Miniature Models (166 Three Bridges Road, Crawley, Sussex). Cast diesel loco body kits for N gauge, various scenic accessories etc.

Chris Leigh (46 Meadow Way, Old Windsor, Berks). DMU detailing and conversion kit, SR EMU and some parts for pre-nationalisation stations.

Lithoplan Model Products (105 Naunton Crescent, Cheltenham, Glos). Full range of signs and transfers for 4mm and 7mm scale BR.

Mabex Products (15 Coastguard Square, Barden Road, Eastbourne, Sussex). 4mm and 2mm scale transfers, destinations and adverts etc.

MTK — Modern Traction Kits (via Crownline Models Ltd, 121 King Street, Maidenhead). 4mm scale kits for diesel locos, DMUs and EMUs.

Post War Prototypes — David J. Parkins (12 De Lisle Road, Bournemouth, Dorset). Range of 7mm scale BR loco kits and coaches.

Precision Paints Co Ltd (PO Box 43, Cheltenham, Glos). Range of BR colours and shades.

Q Kits (8 Kirkwood View, Leeds 16). Range of BR diesel and electric loco kits in 4mm scale.

Ratio Plastic Models Ltd, (Butts Pond, Sturminster Newton, Dorset). Range of signals in 4mm and many accessories in 4mm and 2mm scales.

Spratt and Winkle (19 Forest Road, Chandlers Ford, Eastleigh, Hants). 4mm scale signals and couplings.

Tiny Signs (PO Box 4, Henley-on-Thames, Oxon). Miniature posters and advertisements in 4mm scale.

W & H Models Ltd (14 New Cavendish Street, London W1). Range of modelling tools, kits and general models.

Westdale Coaches & Models (The Old Granary, Bank Street, Bishops Waltham, near Southampton, Hants). Ready-to-run and kits in 7mm scale or coaches also DMUs and EMUs.

Westward Scale Models (Crow Meadow, Kingswood, Wotton-under-Edge, Glos). Conversion and detailing kits for 4mm scale diesel locos.

Right:
Hornby Class 86 electric loco with a rake of Airfix/Mainline Mk 2d coaches running on the 4mm scale garden layout of Don Jones which depicts the operations of the London Midland Region. *Brian Monaghan*